LET YOUR
LEADERSHIP
SPEAK

HOW TO LEAD AND BE HEARD

Rick Barnes • David Coleman • Doug Cureton

Lenny Dave • Nancy Hunter Denney • Randy Haveson

Kathy Humphrey • Will Keim, Ph.D. • Charles Luke Latour, OP

James Malinchak • Joe Martin • Marlon Smith

The Future is Yours to Create! Company
Paxton, Massachusettes

Library of Congress Catalog Card Number: 2002100013

ISBN: 0-9716914-0-1

Bulk rate discounted purchasing is available through contacting the publishing coordinator listed below or by contacting one of the authors.

Edited by Laurie Porter, Rick Barnes and Nancy Hunter Denney
Book Production Coordinators: Nancy Hunter Denney, Rick Barnes and James Malinchak
Layout and Design: Jim Weems, Ad Graphics, Inc.
Cover Design: Jim Weems, Ad Graphics, Inc.
Printing: Central Plains Book Manufacturing, Inc.

For Additional Information:

Publishing Coordinator – Let Your Leadership Speak
The Future is Yours to Create! Company
50 Richards Avenue
Paxton, MA 01612
Toll free: 888-566-7536

First Edition

10 9 8 7 6 5 4 3 2 1

Table of Contents

Introduction

By Nancy Hunter Denney

Remember when all you wanted was to be picked? Whether for the dodge ball game on the playground or by your first grade teacher, it meant something to hear your name called. By shouting, "Over here!" or "Pick me!" you usually increased the odds of being chosen sooner, as opposed to, later. So, you made noise. Didn't matter if you had the skill or the answer, your number one goal was to draw attention to yourself.

As you grew up, your desire to be chosen only changed venues. From the classroom to the boardroom, or from the playground to your field of expertise, you still want to be in the game. You still want to be acknowledged. You still want to participate. Your hand is in the air and your feet are ready to move. No longer in grade school, you now face the question, "If chosen, what are you going to say and what are you are going to do?"

Let Your Leadership Speak is a collection of answers and inspirations. Twelve voices share their perspectives on how to lead and be heard. Throughout each chapter, words of experience speak to specific understandings of leadership or to a specific skill necessary for effective leadership. Rather than presenting a "right" or "wrong" way of leadership, this book offers alternatives.

Look around. Many people are making it to high levels of achievement within—or without—their particular venues of opportunity. Leadership is a means to achieving a goal. It is not the goal. This understanding allows you to recognize that a position of leadership does not define the person. A title is not required. An election is not necessary. When you let *your* leadership speak you intentionally move toward an improved social condition, advance a well planned agenda, or engage in productive collective energies. You become a better person and produce better results. *Your voice is heard.*

Throughout our lives, it becomes clear that not all people believe their voice can be heard. They speak only to themselves or speak negatively in an effort to make themselves appear more favorably to others. Every author in this book represents an individual who strives to walk the walk and talk the talk. Once you take the risk of educating others, inspiring others, and training others, the source of your knowledge can come into question—either out of respect or suspect. Each author has drawn on his or her own experiences to tell a story, make a point or challenge you to act upon your own insights. We are as we appear.

Honored to be included in this group of individuals, I share an example below of just one way we attempt to reach into your heart, mind and soul to make a difference in your potential to lead—regardless of your level of accomplishment, position or experience. The year was 1974. I was a senior in high school and one of the greatest leaders in my life was my English teacher. His name was Mr. Marvin. He cared enough about me—and so many other young adults—to not only speak up, but to speak out. His language was spoken through what he said and what he did. Never could you pass Mr. Marvin in the hallway without his quizzing you on an upcoming vocabulary word. Never would you run a track meet, without looking over and seeing him applauding your efforts.

Senior breakfast was a venue Mr. Marvin used to take an optimistic high-spirited young adult and give her some words to ponder for the rest of her life. How fortunate that I forgot to raise my hand, but he called on me anyway. Mr. Marvin said, "Now, there's one thing you need to remember as you prepare to go out into this world on your own." I stopped stuffing pancakes into my mouth to listen. "Remember, my friend, you might just be right." Then, Mr. Marvin stopped talking and got up. I saw him for the last time at my graduation, for his life was cut tragically short, but I listen to him on a daily basis.

You might just be right. What was that suppose to mean? You might just be right. It has taken me a while to figure out what Mr. Marvin was trying to tell me—in *his own voice*. He said, "Believe." More specifically, he was telling me to trust in my ideas, my values, my goals, my visions, my likes and my dislikes. He was screaming at me in a quiet and knowing voice to lead because my beliefs and my actions, might just be right.

So, there's just one lesson on life and leadership, twelve more can be found if you keep reading. You will also find straight forward "how to" tips and strategies to enhance your current skills. This is a book based on the belief that *you* might just be right. Others may not be ready to listen, yet others may join in your voice. Let your leadership speak volumes and reflect who you are and what you do. This book offers the gift of twelve professional educators devoted to speaking their truth on a daily basis. Take what fits. Adjust as the writing styles change and individual personalities jump off the page. Be open to the practical and the philosophical. But, most importantly, begin to talk. In fact, let your leadership speak!

. . . .

On Leading by Serving

The Voice of Joe Martin

True leaders lead with their hearts,
not with their heads.

As a leader, sometimes you probably feel overworked, underpaid, overstressed, and unappreciated. I can sympathize. As a person responsible for helping others feel good about themselves, I too feel overworked and unappreciated at times. My mother once told me, "You may not always get what you want in life, but thank God you don't always get what you deserve." This golden nugget of wisdom helps me to stay humble and keep a fresh perspective on life. We may indeed feel tired and stressed as leaders, but we should also feel thankful to be in a position that allows us to positively influence the lives of others.

Ironically, this is where the problem of leadership begins. As leaders, we often become so wrapped up in ourselves and in our problems that we lose sight of our true purpose—which is to serve others. Sometimes the toughest lesson in life is our failure to learn the easy ones. Just consider the following simple service lessons we've all been taught since childhood, but often neglect as adults:

- "Give and you shall receive."
- "Treat others the way you want to be treated."
- "Do unto others as you will have them do unto you."

Imagine if we all practiced those three principles. What if every time someone interacted with you, he or she asked the question, *"What can I do for you?"* as opposed to *"What can you do for me?"*

What kind of members would you have on your team? What kind of colleagues would you have in your organization? More importantly, what kind of leader would you become if YOU practiced those three lessons consistently?

Most of the time, you would have a better chance of finding a winning lottery ticket than a true servant leader. Unfortunately, we live in a society that focuses primarily on putting our own needs before the needs of others. In a sense, it's the American way. As a speaker, consultant, and professor, I teach and live by the philosophy that life's choices are quite simple: *get up, give up, or shut up*. We can either choose to *get up* and change our organization; we can choose to *give up* and accept it as it is; or we can choose to just *shut up* and stop complaining about it.

> "*Everyone can be great, because everyone can serve.*"
> – Martin Luther King, Jr.

Service is a *choice*. You can choose either to serve your organization or serve yourself, but the choice is definitely yours to make. Typically, we think of service as an obligation—something we do grudgingly. However, on a deeper level, serving really has little to do with what you do for others; it has more to do with your heart and attitude toward others.

In its purest form, serving others is the epitome of abundance; it lies at the heart of humanity, and it's the secret to all success. George Fraser, author of *Success Runs in Our Race*, says that we were all put here on earth to be "used." That fact alone should raise an eyebrow or two. Who in their right mind wants to be "used"? However, if you take a closer look at that statement, you will see the wisdom behind it. Fraser doesn't suggest that we were intended to be "*misused*" or "*abused*," but to be "*used*." After all, if you aren't being used, wouldn't that imply that you're perhaps "*use-less*"?

As with service, leadership is also a choice. And when it comes to servant leadership, you can choose to be underutilized; you can choose not to be used at all; or you can even choose to use others.

True servant leaders allow themselves (their gifts, talents, and abilities) to be properly used for the benefit of others and the organization as a whole. It's as simple as that. The greater your responsibility to lead, the greater your responsibility to serve.

"To whom much is given, much is required (Luke 12:48);
the greatest among you must also be your
greatest servant (Matthew 20:24);
love your neighbor as you do yourself (Matthew 22:39);
give and you shall receive (Mark 4:24)."

If you study any of the world's most influential leaders, past or present, you will find that one of their most admirable traits is their ability and willingness to serve others. Basically, we're supposed to be in the *"giving,"* not the *"receiving"* business. The process gets confusing and frustrating when we try to rearrange the natural order of things.

For instance, I grew up in one of the toughest inner-city ghettos in Miami, Florida. I was influenced by many so-called "leaders," from gang members to drug dealers. The lessons I learned on the streets about leadership were cold and brutal:

- "Do it to others BEFORE they do it to you."
- "Do it to others UNTIL you get caught."
- "Do it to others while nobody's looking."

In later life, I learned from watching servant leaders in action that there is a name for someone who takes without giving. Can you guess what it is? That's right, it's called "a thief." Although the majority of people I knew growing up in the hood were "takers," not all of them were incarcerated. I later discovered that there are a lot of "thieves in training." These are the people who usually go undetected by law enforcement. You might even know a few of them. If they're on the job, they're always complaining about what their boss or company is NOT doing for them or NOT paying them. If they're in a relationship, they are always complaining about what their mate is NOT doing for them. If they're in the classroom, they're always complaining about what their teacher or institution is NOT doing for them or NOT teaching them. I think you get the picture.

In a sense, these people can be considered "thieves," which means they take without giving. When you think about it, the only reason why most managers, supervisors, and employees aren't in jail is because there's no law against what they're stealing from their employer. The same could be said for people in relationships. If there's no deposit, you should not expect a return.

If you don't believe me, try visiting your local bank and requesting a withdrawal of $10,000. You will be surprised how cordial the bank teller will be as he politely asks for your account number. When you respond that you neither have an account with their bank, nor do you have $10,000 deposited in any bank, you'll be lucky if he doesn't call security to escort you out of the building. NO DEPOSIT means NO WITHDRAWAL!

Contrary to popular belief, leadership isn't about the number of people you lead, but rather about the number of people who are willing to follow you when it counts. So how do you do it? How can you put more service into your leadership, thus increasing your effectiveness? It's easy: you **get more** out of your leadership potential by **simply giving more** to your organization and its members.

On the surface, we all *give* in some capacity, but we don't all *serve*. We give our time, money, and energy to causes and projects every single day, but it's not the same as serving. You can spend time with me without becoming emotionally involved. You can give money to my cause and not really believe in it. And guess what, you can show up for work every day without taking a single day off and still not be a productive leader. Each of these cases reflects giving but not serving.

In our work place, in our communities and in our homes, we don't need more "givers," we need more "servers." When you give your money, time and energy to your organization, never forget the most important ingredient...your heart. Giving your heart is much different from giving your resources. Giving your heart is an investment; it's also a serious commitment.

As a leader, you're required to show up for work on time, spend money (i.e., budget), and work hard enough so you won't get fired. That's the minimum required to keep a position. But when it comes to servant leadership, no organization can require or force you to put your heart into your work. That's an individual choice that you must make every day. Unfortunately, we have too many leaders serving from the head up rather than from the heart up. Are you a giver or are you a server?

I've designed a list of questions I believe you and every member of your team should ask and answer. I've done a longer version of this exercise with more than a thousand managers and administrators in an effort to help them lead with more passion. This Q & A exercise is simple, but revealing, requiring only honesty on your part. If you're really a courageous leader, you might even suggest that your team discuss their individual answers as a group. Here are a few questions to ask:

Do your responsibilities give you more headaches or more heartaches?

If you are a true leader, your position should give you more heartaches (i.e., the pain of not seeing an objective reached, a team member not being empowered, or the organization not improving) than headaches. As painful as it may sound, heartaches should be the reasons WHY you became a leader in the first place...to make a difference.

Your sincere passion to improve the lives of others, build the organization and instill a sense of pride are the ingredients of true leadership. Heartaches give you the drive to keep getting up after you've been knocked down by the headaches. Trust me, there's always room in your life for the organizational headaches (i.e., paperwork, bureaucracy, phone calls, apathy, etc.), but space should be limited.

Would you continue to serve your organization even if you weren't recognized for your contribution?

Everyone likes to feel appreciated, but that's not always possible. If you feel you always have to be praised for your efforts, you might want to reevaluate your purpose in being a leader. Whether you receive a pat on the back or a kick in the butt, the satisfaction you get from being a leader should come from knowing that you've made a great effort and you're leading with integrity.

Do you get more excited about going to organizational planning meetings or missing them?

Believe it or not, you should be excited about attending meetings. A meeting is an opportunity to launch new ideas, evaluate old ones, and discuss the potential impact of your organization. Unless your team is wasting time in meetings, you should be pumped up about participating. This is a chance to rally the troops and get everyone to renew their commitment to the goals and objectives of your organization.

If serving others was a crime, would there be enough evidence on your job to convict you?

In this country, you are innocent until proven guilty. But in this particular case, you want to be found guilty of serving too much. Start compiling your evidence; who knows, one day you might be asked to prove your case. The last thing you want to have to do when asked "What have you done for us lately?" is plead the fifth.

Is my attitude helping or hurting the organization?

It's so easy to identify what's wrong with the weakest links in our organization. However, if you truly want to improve your organization, you must (and should) start with improving yourself. The largest room in your house should always be your room for improvement. Start today by identifying some of the blind spots in your own personality and commit yourself to strengthening those areas. It's almost impossible to improve yourself and NOT improve your organization.

So, how did you do? Are you serving your organization or are you just serving your time? During this Q and A exercise, if you discover that either you or someone in your organization is doing more taking than serving, here are your options:

Option 1: Resolve.

If you want to remain in the organization and your actions and attitude have caused pain to others, admit your misguided motives by publicly apologizing. This will not be an easy thing to do. However, if you're sincere, you will heal some unspoken wounds and at the same time, earn the respect of your team.

Option 2: Reprioritize.

If you want to remain in the organization and you've successfully managed to camouflage some of your selfish motives, simply reprioritize and refocus your efforts. Commit yourself to putting your organization's needs above your own. Don't just tell your members what to do or what you plan to do, show them.

Option 3: Resign.

Lastly, if you know that you or another member of your organization will have a better chance at winning a wrestling match with a crocodile than letting go of his or her selfish ways, graciously resign from the position. Until you realize that your own needs will only be met to the degree to which you meet the needs of others, you may actually serve your organization better by leaving it.

FIVE SERVICE ENHANCEMENT STRATEGIES

You've just given yourself a service check-up from the "heart up." You've also been given the opportunity to consider three options or courses of behavior depending on your discoveries. The following five sure-fire service strategies will help you maximize your leadership potential. I've coached organizations on these service strategies and used them myself. They have produced amazing results.

Service Strategy #1: Turn the Tables

In order to demonstrate your commitment to leadership, you have to give more than lip service; you have to give yourself something to lose. In other words, you need to raise your level of influence among your team members by demonstrating that you are in this position for the long haul. If you're giving only time, money and energy to your organization, you haven't really started serving. As I mentioned earlier, your organization will benefit from your contributions whether you give willingly or reluctantly. But I'm challenging you to go the extra mile by giving in a way that shows you're serious about your role as a leader.

For example, whenever I'm asked to speak, train or consult for an organization, inevitably the issue of price comes up. And as most speakers and consultants know, we're probably going to get paid whether we do a good job or a bad job. However, to set myself apart as a leader and as a committed speaker, consultant and trainer, I've written into every contract that if the meeting or event planner is not completely satisfied with the results I produce, their organization gets my services absolutely free of charge. In fact, I've even gone a step further. If the client isn't completely satisfied, in addition to donating my services for free, I will also make a $500 contribution to the organization's favorite charity.

If I don't make an impact with my message, I will at least make an impact with my money. This simple gesture holds me accountable to my client and improves my performance and preparation. That's what I mean by giving yourself something to lose. Think about it this way. What would you think of an employee or colleague who told you that if she didn't produce the results she promised, you could keep her paycheck until she did? I don't want you to expect it from others; I want you to expect it of yourself.

Service Strategy #2: Make a Down Payment

One of the best ways to get yourself in the servant leadership mentality is to serve your organization as if someone you loved was going to receive the benefits. This particular strategy is highly effective if you can convince yourself of its merits. You have to really think about it for a minute. Most of the time, we do things (even the right things) if we see a direct personal benefit or reward in it. This, in and of itself, isn't bad. However, if you were to adopt the mindset that everything you did in your organization directly or indirectly affected someone you love (i.e. your child, parent, or mate), you would see a significant change in your attitude toward service.

For example, teachers are arguably among the lowest paid professionals in the United States. Therefore, it's not surprising to hear so many problems and complaints concerning education in America. "Morale is low, teachers are discouraged, the competency level of teachers has fallen, etc." However, the ones who suffer the most are our children. As teachers debate and legislators resist, students are slowly falling through the cracks. What if every teacher, every administrator and every legislator asked themselves, "How would I teach students, lead school districts, and pay educators if I knew the choice would directly impact MY child?" Do you think we would see some changes? And how soon do you think those changes would take place? As servant leaders, we need to make down payments on future benefits. It's definitely worth the investment, at least for the ones we love.

Service Strategy #3: Go Public with It

If you really want to raise your level of influence and affect your members, go public by having organization-wide brainstorming sessions. This is not a new concept, but most organizations and organizational leaders do it the wrong way. Most leaders ask for feedback and input, but at the same time, they want to protect their egos. As a leader, you want to put your ego aside to demonstrate your sincerity concerning your personal and professional development. I do this twice a year with my team, and it continues to produce incredible results. Here's how you do it.

Arrange to meet with all of your key team members (the more the better), and ask them to take out a sheet of paper. Inform them that you're trying to become a more effective leader and that you need their help. Let them know you will ask them a series of questions, and you want them to respond honestly and anonymously on paper. Tell each person to write down the following questions and type out their answers later; they can turn in their typed responses to you at the next meeting. Remember, they are to remain anonymous.

Questions:

1. *All year I've been wanting to complain to (your name) about...*
2. *The one thing I wish (your name) would stop doing as a leader is...*
3. *(Your name) could really improve our organization if he...*
4. *All year I've wanted to praise (your name) on his ability to...*
5. *The one thing I hope (your name) will keep doing as a leader is...*
6. *One reason I would recommend that someone work for (your name) is because...*

As a leader, this insightful exercise helps you to uncover what's not working, what you can do to improve it, and how your members feel about your leadership abilities. Obviously, it's not an exercise for the faint of heart. But it's absolutely necessary if you want to become the best leader you can be. Trust me, if you're willing to make the necessary changes, the results will be well worth the initial pain.

Service Strategy #4: Let Them Catch You in the Act

If you want to be an effective servant leader, you must lead by example rather than by exerting power. I've found in my various work positions that one of the quickest ways to motivate someone to do something is to let them catch you doing it first.

> *"Nothing corrupts absolutely like absolute power."*
> – Abraham Lincoln

One of the best managers I've ever had the pleasure of working for was a man named Larry. He was one of the company's youngest district managers (26 years old at the time), and had been well known for his record-breaking sales accomplishments. In less than four years with our company (a Fortune 500 company), Larry had emerged as one of the top-producing sales reps in our company's history. Even with his impressive track record, because of his age, most of our staff did not respect Larry when he was chosen to lead our district. In addition to being young, he was one of the highest paid, and he was in charge. He knew his leadership position would be questioned.

Although Larry wasn't particularly charismatic or assertive, he eventually earned the respect of everyone on our staff. Never had I seen a person say so little (as a leader) and accomplish so much in such a short period of time. Our office became one of the most productive in the district. How did he turn our office around and win the respect of our staff? Easy. We always caught him in the act.

Despite the fact that he was one of the highest paid managers in our company, he always showed up for work before anyone else. He always left later than everyone else. In fact, in my two years with the company, I never actually saw him show up for work or leave—he was just always there. Whenever he suggested a better way of doing things, he always provided evidence that he himself had tried it first.

One day, I was frustrated with my prospecting efforts when Larry came by my office to pep me up. When I questioned how anyone in their right mind could deal with the rejection and monotony of prospecting, he made a few calls himself (which all resulted in rejections); then he gave me a copy of his old prospecting books that tracked the number of calls made, rejections received, and subsequent appointments he booked as a rep. I was amazed. His persistence was so impressive that I committed myself to prospecting until I reached my appointment goals (every day). In less than a year, I became the top producing sales rep in our office. I give all of the credit to a boss who wasn't afraid to let us catch him in the act of doing exactly what he expected from us.

Service Strategy #5: Be a Genie

The fifth and final strategy has been consistently effective for me on the job, in the classroom, and in the boardroom. I call it "The Genie." Specifically, find out exactly what your employee, teammate or staff person wants, then show them how to get it in the context of the organization's goals and objectives. This strategy is at the pinnacle of servant leadership: putting other people's needs before your own. But don't think for a second that servant leadership makes you someone's doormat. On the contrary, a sincere effort to help others get what they want will make them forever indebted to you. It's quite simple and quite effective.

When I worked for the federal government, I had a co-worker who despised her job. Although I wasn't her immediate supervisor, as her friend, I advised her many times either to change jobs or quit. Her disdain for her job showed in her work and her attitude toward others. When she refused to quit because of financial obligations, I tried repeatedly to get her to see the negative impact she was having on other staff members and our customers. She refused to listen.

Then I tried a new approach, one that management had never thought of employing. I took her out to lunch one day and asked her about her passion and ambitions. Although we had worked together for a couple of years, I never saw her express so much enthusiasm as when she talked about her passion to teach and train others.

I immediately took this newfound knowledge and started searching for opportunities within our division for her to exercise those talents. Remember, I was not her supervisor, but her job (and effectiveness) directly affected mine. I sent her information about job openings in training and staff development, articles from magazines, books written by some of the top training professionals, etc. In other words, I showed her numerous ways to get what she wanted. I even showed her how she could utilize her training talents in her current position (a job that she thought was unrelated to training).

All in all, this strategy worked. Her attitude improved, her performance improved, and her customer service dramatically improved. Although she still didn't like her job, she didn't feel as trapped as she once had. However, for "The Genie" strategy to work, you have to have a sincere interest in others. You need to be resourceful and willing to listen (even when they whine). But when you think about it, isn't that what a "servant leader" should be?

> *"The best exercise for the human heart is a sincere*
> *effort to reach down and help lift up others."*
> *– Former President George Bush*

Truth be told, the reason why most leaders don't serve is because there aren't enough good examples to follow. Your leadership legacy should be a map for future generations, not a detour sign. If we're not getting enough out of our organizations, then we're not serving enough. As leaders, we can only take people as far as we've traveled ourselves. So ask yourself some tough questions...

- *What can you do to better serve your organization?*

- *Are you serving with your heart or your head?*

- *Are you clear about the role your leadership should play in your organization?*

- *Do your actions speak louder than your words?*

- *If you were only paid based on what you've given to others through service, how long could you survive on the paycheck?*

- *Will your leadership legacy be one of service?*

*In all you do, lead and serve with
purpose, passion, and power!*

CHAPTER SUMMARY

❑ By understanding the importance of servant leadership and how it impacts your organization, you will be a more effective leader.

❑ Distinguish between "giving to" and "serving" your organization.

❑ Correct a self-serving attitude and regain the respect of your team.

❑ Get more out of your organization, your team, and yourself with five proven service strategies.

❑ You can become the type of leader your team will "choose" to follow.

. . . .

2

On Leading with Charisma
The Voice of Nancy Hunter Denney

"You make a living by what you get.
You make a life by what you give."
— Winston Churchill

"Don't mis-underestimate me!" came the male voice from across the room. Powerful words. Convincing words. Wrong words. Normally, when I'm in the middle of executing my packing ritual—which includes turning on CNN for background noise—I focus only on making sure that everything in my suitcase matches. (When you're 500 miles away from home, it's not a good time to discover you've packed your 8-year-old-daughter's underwear instead of your own or that you'll have to take your morning run wearing two left foot sneakers.) But there I stood, dumbfounded. For "Don't mis-underestimate me!" was being spoken by the President of the United States.

That was then… before the world change. That was when making fun of the President of the United States was all part of the game, even a sport. Pointing out the bloopers and blunders of those who sit in the Oval Office seemed to take up significant air time one might think better used with "real" news. I admit to being amused and amazed at how far people could rise in this world despite their lack of common sense or non-charismatic speaking presence. But, the world changed. The President, when faced with unthinkable challenges, found the presence he needed to lead. In front of my very eyes, the leader of the free world went from stumbling on words to speaking from the heart. He went from being uncomfortable behind the podium to instilling comfort in those who listened. Yes, the world changed.

We all make mistakes. We make errors in language that detract from our potential to positively influence or impress others. For example, we mix up tenses, occasionally forget that "good" is not an adverb (i.e. I did good…) or start a sentence with "Umm." At times, it's not even what we say or don't say that makes us less than charismatic. Maybe you know what it's like to be told that your shirt tail is sticking out of your fly or that the price tag from your obviously brand-new $800 suit is still dangling from the sleeve. You were so close to pulling it all together. You were so close to making a great impression. What went wrong?

There are many sure signs of missing your mark. People are perceptive. When you feel uncomfortable about the kind of impression you made or your inability to lead, be assured that other people also noticed. That's a simple fact of life and leadership. Actions are powerful communicators of your sense of self. Part of being human is to make mistakes in our behavior or communications that significantly detract from our ability to inspire, persuade, impress, lead or pull it all together. Others may forgive our mistakes, but that doesn't mean they will forget them.

Several years ago, on a flight back from Chicago, I sat next to the CEO of a well-known Fortune 500 company. He appeared very agitated. After we introduced ourselves and talked briefly, I asked him how his day had gone. He sighed and said, "I missed it." Not understanding him, I probed further. He became more agitated, but luckily not with me. Finally, he looked at me and said, "I was brilliant. I was prepared. I gave one of my most powerful speeches to date." Then there was a very long pause before he concluded, "I had toilet paper stuck to the bottom of my shoe the entire time I was on stage." End of conversation. I changed the subject.

My flight companion, a very successful leader who has graced the cover of many national magazines and was most likely paid six figures for his speech, knew that his credibility had been compromised because of the trail of toilet paper that had followed him on and off stage. With time, I'm sure that the sting of his mishap diminished—or at least I hope it did—but one doesn't reach his level of leadership without knowing that actions speak louder than words. He knew he had missed "it."

Leaders are expected to be poised and authoritative. They are called upon to express ideas with clarity, inspire others to follow and be perceptive to potential sources of resistance. They are expected, for example, to take their position of influence responsibly in times of national crisis and speak in a manner that instills trust. Leaders need to be charismatic to lead effectively. Your ability to lead is directly related to your ability to attract others to your vision or purpose and to instill trust in those you lead. This ability is what I call your "charismatic style."

Every day, wherever you go and whatever you do, you are observed, judged and evaluated. You send "personal vibrations" to your employer, friends, potential clients, partner, dry cleaners and even to complete strangers. Your actions (and inactions) affect all that happens around you, or fails to happen. Charisma is the aura that accompanies you, a personal magnetic force that attracts others to your leadership style and makes them receptive to your ideas. Simply put, charisma is the "it" you wish you had or admire in others.

Do you have "it?" Ask yourself the following questions. Does your very presence at the water cooler literally part the waters? Do you wonder why no one wants to stick around and "pick your brain" after one of your well-prepared presentations? Are you envious of how other leaders of organizations appear to be "people magnets," always walking and talking with others, and never escorted into the restroom by fewer than three people? And here's the hardest question: Have you ever been congratulated for your brilliant strategy and in the same breath been told that someone else—not you—will be the one to share it at the meeting? Ouch.

Charisma is a silent force that overrides competing
influences for attention and makes
you appealing to others.

Charismatic leadership requires the consistent use of specific behaviors, language and gestures, varying them as necessary to fit the appropriate audience or environment. No matter what your age, educational background, work experience, economic status or employment ranking, you can become a better leader by working on your charismatic style. Moreover, charismatic leadership has the potential to raise the standard for behavior in your immediate environment. When your co-workers are treated with respect (i.e. "Good morning, how are you?" versus "Is my memo typed yet?"), they feel better about themselves and their organization; they work with greater energy and begin to look to you as a leader because of your style, not your stature.

There is no doubt—or coincidence—that leaders deemed to be charismatic make more sales, produce more, get elected to more public offices and receive more invitations to speak publicly. Charismatic individuals are asked to head up teams and sit on committees. Bottom line: they get noticed by others in positions to provide them with even more opportunities to get noticed. In short, charismatic leaders advance to leadership positions because they put themselves there.

Throughout this book, you will repeatedly be told that many traits of leadership can be learned. Such is the case with charisma. Despite the fact that there are those who appear to just have "it"— the big smile, the George Clooney twinkle in the eye, a commanding presence—in reality, you can do much to enhance your ability to attract others to your messages, missions and moments. Below you will find six practical tips to help you enhance your charismatic style and make you a more effective leader. The key to each tip's success is how often you incorporate it into your daily routine.

CHARISMA BUILDING TIPS

Tip #1: Use a Mirror

Stand in front of a mirror. Talk to it. Rehearse your next conversation in front of it. Then ask yourself how you would describe your personal presence. Studies indicate that we use gestures, mannerisms, movements, eye contact and facial expressions to transmit between 60 - 80% of all of our communication. Before your next committee or board meeting, get in front of a mirror and see how you sit. Is your back straight? Do you hold your head high? Poised posture makes you look more confident. So, sit up!

As a professional speaker, I practice every speech in front of a mirror. I must confess, I scare myself at times. There are arm gestures that I've trained myself to avoid because they make me look as though I'm ready to take flight. I've actually seen myself tilt my head while making a point instead of looking straight ahead. The result making me appear as if I don't even believe what I'm saying! One of the reasons personal coaches are so popular among industry leaders is that coaches verbalize what the mirror sees. But you don't need a coach to tell you that you shouldn't point while making a point. All you really need to become more charismatic is what you already have: common sense.

Observe yourself standing in front of the mirror. Watch yourself speak. Write down what you like and don't like. Experiment with different hand motions to support your points, turn your head in certain ways and most important, try smiling. As you practice your current communication style, consider the following facts about non-verbal communication:

- Crossing your legs while standing is interpreted as insecurity.
- Crossing your arms (or putting a shoulder forward) is a "blocking" message and communicates superiority or insincerity.
- Maintaining eye contact communicates self-confidence and interest in the other person's thoughts.
- Sitting upright in a chair shows confidence. Posture matters.
- Nodding can be a sign of agreement or paying attention.
- Initiating a handshake signals respect for the other person.

Tip #2: Take Social Risks

If you are serious about enhancing your charisma, then it's time to get out of your zone of comfort. You need to practice being more charismatic with complete strangers before trying out the new you on those who will anticipate certain language and actions from you.

For example, go join a group or organization where no one knows you. Then, stop talking! As a new member, sit quietly and observe what others are doing and saying. Regardless of your current leadership role, no one needs to know your position of authority. Let them experience your personality and read the non-verbal signals you send out. Ironically, charismatic individuals tend more to encourage and prompt others to talk rather than to dominate the conversation themselves. So, show up then shut up!

> *"Don't talk while I'm interrupting!"*
> *– Tony Alessandra, Ph.D.*

Consider experimenting within your current leadership capacities. One of the greatest ways to take a risk is to invite others to take a risk. In other words, ask more probing questions and open-ended questions. Seek out the ideas of others. You will always make more friends and connect better with people when you invite them to talk about themselves. What's the risk? You then have to respond to the unknown and unanticipated. You will instantly have to learn the art of spontaneous conversation, listening without judgment and acting on the communication. You will also benefit from following up. For example, write a note, make a call or jot down a name with notes about your conversation. Remember, go out of your zone of familiarity (i.e. talking about yourself) and open yourself up to the lives and ideas of others.

This sounds easy. It's not. I often have to remind myself to turn the conversation back to the individual(s) with whom I am speaking. To do so, I often rely on a trigger phrase, "Tell me more about (fill in the blank)." Remove the "I" and replace it with "What about you?" Demonstrating your own self-importance by monopolizing the conversation is a charisma killer.

> *"You can make more friends in two weeks than you can*
> *in two years by genuinely getting interested in other people*
> *than trying to get other people interested in you."*
> *– Dale Carnegie*

Asking for more from your daily interactions—especially with strangers—can bring marvelously unexpected results. How often have you heard the phrase, "It's a small world?" I'll never forget my experience at a meeting several years ago, when I almost missed one of the most interesting conversations of my life simply because I didn't feel like playing. After giving a speech, I actively sought a table that had no one sitting at it. After I had enjoyed only a few minutes of peace, a gentleman came along, pulled out a chair, and sat down with me. I smiled. He smiled. We stared at each other. Breaking the silence, I asked him if he had also been speaking at this conference. "Yes, Ma'am," he replied. In fact, every question I asked him was answered with a monosyllabic affirmative or negative, followed by a smile. Our conversation was like a game of Twenty Questions and I was it.

Eventually, I discovered that he was an expert on the topic of security. Intrigued, I asked, trying for humor, "Oh, security as in door locks or as in guarding the president?" "The president," he answered. Being ever so witty, I then said, "Oh, like you were the president's personal bodyguard or something?" He smiled and said, "That would be correct, Ma'am." An hour later, I was still enthralled by his stories about working as a CIA agent—at least the stories he could share without having to kill me. You just never know.

Your pursuit of charisma might just lead to the same array of fascinating conversations and discoveries that I have enjoyed. Since I have begun to enhance my charismatic style of communication and take active risks, I have built significant relationships with people I might not have previously met. As a leader, you will have numerous opportunities to enlarge and diversify your friendships, contacts and work relationships. But, you need to make the first, second and third moves! And don't forget to follow up.

Charismatic leadership involves more than
the communication of your ideas—
it is your ideas.

Tip #3: Read More and Think More

Get smarter. Small talk and superficial comments result in shallow relationships and communications. To become more charismatic you must also make yourself more interesting by knowing something other than sports scores, the weather forecast or today's stock market activity. Treat yourself to the top ten best sellers and stack them up on your nightstand. Then open your mind by opening a book not normally of your genre. Not all female executives, for example, want to talk about domestic issues—a common assumption by male executives. Not all male employees, for example, want to discuss sports. Do you have an assortment of topics to which you can converse?

Subscribe to a major newspaper that introduces stories based upon content, not commercial appeal. Listen to public radio. In a short amount of time, you will find yourself with an enhanced awareness of what is happening in the world—not just in your immediate surroundings. Despite an impulse I know all too well, try to avoid bringing up the last episode of West Wing. When you can knowledgeably discuss the Middle East peace process or weave information about the latest Pulitzer Prize winners into your conversation, you become more interesting.

By expanding your intellectual horizons, you also expand your vocabulary. The charismatic individual embraces a large vocabulary, understanding that words are an important means of exhibiting your intellect and sense of self. As a leader, the more advanced your vocabulary, the more magnetic your message. Learn one new word every week. Listen to audio-tapes on the way to work, use vocabulary calendars, or post a new word with its definition in your *Palm Pilot*, then try to use it for seven days straight. Read the dictionary! Write down the words you learn and test yourself on a regular basis.

*You're never out of school when you
are trying to be more charismatic.*

Tip #4: Arrive First and Leave Last

One of the greatest ways to overestimate your importance and destroy any chance you have of being a charismatic leader is to be rude. Yet, when you become a leader, it's often not due to intent, but to the demands of a hectic schedule that you run from one meeting to another or have to juggle a multitude of obligations. Nonetheless, charismatic energy is a spark waiting to be ignited, not a flame ready to burn whatever lies in its path. When you are one of the first ones to arrive at a meeting or event, you communicate anticipation, security, a willingness to participate and your commitment to the group. It shows respect for those who arrive after you.

So, add a fifteen minute window to both ends of your engagements as you record them in your daily planner or as your assistant includes them on your calendar. Be known as a leader who will take the time to make others feel important. It is often before and after meetings that you learn the most about participants, their ideas and how they really feel about the topic under discussion. Only naïve leaders believe that a meeting's agenda is the one they set.

The way I see it, there are three kinds of people in this world. The ones who see the glass as half empty. The ones who see it as half full. And those—like the leaders—who are too busy looking for a water fountain to notice how much water is in the glass.

Tip #5: Look for the Water Fountain

Attitude plays a vital role in the kind of energy a leader communicates. The charismatic individual is the one who finds solutions and represents hope, direction, guidance and faith. As a motivational speaker, I am not about the glass being half empty or half full. I am about the search for a water fountain! I encourage you to exert your energies toward solutions and away from blame or negative talk. Avoid criticizing others, despite their failures or mistakes, and find a way to praise those who meet your expectations. The only people attracted by negative energy are those who share negative attitudes.

Remember! Your personal magnetism is the degree to which one force will work against another force to produce results. You control the type of force put out there.

Give one compliment an hour. This isn't all that easy. It's also not all that hard. Once again, I encourage you to experiment on complete strangers first. Then, once you appear to be sounding sincere (as I hope you will be, anyway) try one compliment a day with the people you see regularly. Too many at once may suggest something's not right or that your motives are to be questioned. Ease into the process of seeing what's working, not what's broken. Positive energy will only create more positive energy—and that's what charisma is all about in the first place.

"I often quote myself, it adds such spice to my conversations."

– George Bernard Shaw

Tip #6: Pursue the Podium

To be a charismatic leader, you must become comfortable speaking publicly. As a leader you will inevitably find yourself in a position to influence others, share ideas, entertain, welcome, inform, inspire and so on. With practice, you will become relaxed in both formal and informal settings where the focus is on you. As a professional speaker, it is my belief that the only difference between a good speaker and a bad speaker is self-confidence. In other words, my number one tip for effective public speaking is to believe in your own ability. Below are a few tips on how to enhance your public speaking skills:

- Seize as many opportunities to speak in front of others as you can.

- Take a public speaking course.

- Write a speech with five or fewer main points, then spend five times as long as it took you to write the speech practicing it in front of the mirror. Not only will this technique shorten your speeches, it will also make your delivery more dynamic.

- Never read a speech verbatim. Make an outline and refer to your notes.

- Share personal stories to back up your points.

- Use other resources (i.e., <u>The Speaker's Source Book</u>, <u>Chicken Soup for the (fill in the blank) Soul</u>, <u>The World Almanac</u>, etc.) when preparing a speech to add interesting quotes, facts or brief stories. Be sure to cite the source and make what you quote relevant to your topic.

- Never introduce yourself before a speech. Write your own introduction and give it to someone else with enough time for them to practice it.

- Open and close your comments with a "hook"—a joke, poem or quote—that lets the audience know you are returning to where you began as a means of concluding your remarks. This hook takes the audience full circle.

We have also come full circle in our brief discussion about how to be a more charismatic leader. You have been exposed to six behavioral changes that will require you to adjust your attitude in order to implement them. Are you willing to move ahead? Are you willing to incorporate these strategies into your every day? I've heard many leaders talk about how they wish they had "it." You, as the leader, define your own personality, purpose and the manner in which you will lead. You've already got "it." Now you want to make what you've got more appealing to others.

Maybe you do not aspire to be the leader of the free world—or maybe you do. The world changes and along with it the expectations people have for their leaders. Maybe we will return to a day when the president's grammatical mistakes will end up broadcast to millions on CNN. Maybe there will be a time when people won't have a desire to judge your every word, sentence, or notice your every action—or inaction. But, if you are called to make a difference, such things usually go with the territory. You can choose to raise your personal standard of appearance, for instance, or you can confess that you have no where else to go. My hunch? If you are taking the time to read this book, you are a dedicated individual looking to move an agenda forward, advance a social cause, or lead an organization or company. You are seeking ways to enhance your charismatic style so you can be a more effective communicator. Am I right? After all, the price you pay for implementing the six strategies above will be directly proportional to the amount of change you are inspired to create. I have seen these strategies take leaders to new levels and they can do the same for you... but only if you don't "mis-underestimate" my words.

"How you spend your time is the only true measurement of your priorities in life."

CHAPTER SUMMARY

❑ Charisma is a personal magnetism resulting from forces working in opposition to each other.

❑ Leadership is the result of learnable skills. Individuals can change behaviors and attitudes to enhance their charismatic styles.

❑ Good communication skills are essential in order to attract individuals to your ideas.

❑ Six strategies for enhancing one's charismatic style include enlarging your vocabulary, taking risks, doing more public speaking, arriving early and leaving late, exuding only positive energy and reading more while thinking more.

❑ The President of the United States makes mistakes, too. At least you know that yours probably won't appear on CNN.

3

On Team Spirit

The Voice of Doug Cureton

I played on my fifth-grade baseball team. Participation was mandatory at recess, so I didn't have much choice. As a heavyset—let's just be authentic from the start and say "fat"—kid, I was always one of the last players picked for the team, the recreational equivalent of the end cut of bologna in the deli case. Although I wasn't conscious of it at the time, the selection process definitely shaped my attitude and my attitude definitely shaped my performance on the team. Left field was designated as the position where I could cause the least harm, so that was my permanent assignment. An occasional stray dog wandered onto the field to keep me company and help me count the dandelions. Like me, they were always there. No matter how many of us trampled on them or how many high-fly pop-ups I dropped to flatten their golden yellow blooms, they bounced back. For the most part, playing left field kept my embarrassment to a minimum. I know now that I may have been ON the team, but I had no team spirit.

Attitude shapes spirit, especially team spirit. Mark Davis was my friend and the captain of our team. Although his selection skills left something to be desired as far as I was concerned, his encouragement was nonetheless at times truly inspiring. Especially when it was time for me to be up at bat. I feared this part of the game the most. All attention focused on me and me alone, as I was ripped from my secluded harbor in left field and forced into the raw exposure of home plate. The entire outfield, even my equally heavy counterpart in left field, moved in to the infield as I walked to the plate. Jeers, not cheers rang out as I took a few practice swings. Inevitably, I almost always struck out.

Then one day, Mark came over to me as I stood looking nervously at the pitcher and said, "I want you to put your weight into the ball and knock it over their heads." Your weight. With that single reference to what I considered to be the source of all of my troubles, Mark gave me both confidence and a focus. He reminded me how to hold the bat and continued to coach me on how I could make my weight a part of that bat. I am not sure anymore exactly what he said that made me get it; it was like that first moment when your bike magically holds you up without the training wheels. All I can remember is that I hit that ball farther than I had ever hit any ball—out to kiss, not crush, my resilient dandelion fans. Thanks to Mark's guidance and my newfound confidence, I had my first home run and my first taste of team spirit. My "teammates" and I talked about that home run the rest of the day. For me, this particular memory stands out as the moment when I first felt like a true member of a team. I wasn't just ON the team anymore; I MATTERED to the team.

> "Spirit: The intangible part of your consciousness
> that can soar or plummet depending upon your daily
> interactions with individuals or your environment."
> – Oprah Winfrey

The Controversy of Spirit

Exactly where spirit is located and when it is present is sometimes hotly—and in my opinion, unnecessarily—debated. Whether it lies in your heart, your soul, your head or that elusive place that only you can define, your spirit is an animating force for creativity, productivity and community. As a leader, encouraging the manifestation of spirit among the members of your organization is a dynamic part of your motivational toolkit for building an inspired and enthusiastic team.

One of the greatest challenges you, as well as, other leaders must face today is the reality that some individuals don't believe that spirit matters on a team. As many participants in some of the mandatory trainings I have conducted have so eloquently put it, "This team building crap is all well and good, but I've got a job to do TODAY!" The pressure to get the job done as quickly and efficiently as possible has led many team members to minimize the need to focus on spirit. This attitude ignores the fact that many time-consuming interruptions during the work day can be directly attributed to a lack of team cohesion and cooperation.

Point #1: A leader is responsible for modeling and engendering a positive spirit in their organization.

Today's leaders have contributed to this skepticism about the value of spirit. The prevailing attitude among many Americans is that our leaders are ethically, morally and spiritually corrupt; it's not what you know, they maintain, but who you know and how you play the system that will ultimately determine the value of your leadership. To address this crisis of confidence, it is important for us to clarify the distinction between politically motivated decision-making and authentic leadership. Some politicians are wonderful leaders who selflessly serve their constituents in order to bring about beneficial gains for their respective communities. As a result, they are viewed as true leaders. They choose to use their knowledge, resources and human capital to invest in and encourage others to participate in the process of leadership.

Today's dependency on technology has also contributed to a declining team spirit within organizations, offices, communities and relationships. For instance, "You've Got Mail!" has replaced "Good morning!" as the first greeting we hear each day. Our growing dependence on e-mail, pagers and *Palm Pilots* is threatening to replace the art of conversation, lessening the amount of time your team members interact directly with one another. Although they are sometimes more efficient in communicating a single, important focused message, these technologies were NOT designed to replace the in-depth conversations often required to elucidate information for the team. Without the non-verbal cues—vocal inflection and intonation, body language and facial expression—that we depend upon to convey the nuances of personal interaction, a great deal of the meaning of communication is lost on-line. So, as a leader you will want to turn off the technology and turn on genuine conversation.

Point #2: Interpersonal communication is the lifeblood of spirit.

Diversity and Spirit

One holiday season, as our staff was trying to determine who would work on Christmas Eve, I was pegged as the favorite candidate. "Doug has no family," my co-workers said, referring to the fact that I was neither married nor a parent. In truth, I did have a family: of parents, brothers, sisters, nieces and nephews. I did not mind having to work, as Christmas Eve is one of the quietest days at the office, but the assumption that I "had no family" not only challenged my spirit but also my willingness to support the needs of my team. Genuine support and appreciation for the various needs of your team requires intentional understanding of the diverse backgrounds that each of the members brings to the organization. From this understanding, the true leader creates opportunities for celebration by incorporating inclusionary practices—"Who would be WILLING to work Christmas Eve?" with an on-going philosophy of valuing the individual. However, creating the spirit of valuing and appreciating our diversity is just the starting point. This is a very involved process that includes, but is not limited to, defining specific policies and procedures for inclusion, conducting formal training that focuses on diversity issues for the organization and continual modeling of inclusionary attitudes and behaviors by all members of the group.

Point #3: Leaders empower members to empathically understand, appreciate and celebrate the diversity of all members as a foundation for a authentic and valuing organization.

One of the most challenging teams on which I ever worked was at the Providence Performing Arts Center in Rhode Island. I was hired as the House Manager to replace a person who had essentially killed the team spirit of the volunteer staff. The theater schedule dictated that we needed approximately 300 volunteer ushers to handle the number of scheduled shows; we were down to just 100. When I met with the head usher to assess the damage, he told me that the previous manager had paid little attention to the needs of the staff and exhibited no gratitude for their contributions. The only reason the head usher staff had agreed to remain was that they received a stipend for their work. They informed me that the volunteers were tired of being berated and ordered around. They wanted to help the theater, but not if they had to continue to work for an ungrateful manager who did not understand the inconvenience of parking downtown, the risk of having their cars vandalized and the value of a thank you at the end of the evening.

After this meeting, I wrote a letter to each of the volunteers expressing my sincere apologies for any mistreatment they had received and assuring them that, indeed, things were going to change. I invited them to a meeting in the theater, with refreshments, where I planned to introduce the new policies and procedures I had instituted for the PPAC Usher Staff. I also requested a raise for the head usher staff. At my opening meeting, I started simply with the words, "thank you." The smiles on the faces of those volunteers told me instantly that we were on our way.

"No man nor women ever put forth a
better effort under a spirit of criticism
than under a spirit of approval."
– Charles Schwaub

During the remainder of my tenure at PPAC, I held thank you receptions for the volunteers and continually assessed their needs by listening to their ideas and concerns after every performance. Max Depree, in his wonderful book, *Leadership as an Art*, reminds us that a leader has three responsibilities: to be a servant, to define reality, and to be grateful enough for the experience of leadership to remember to say "thank you."

Point #4: Leaders make intentional efforts to nurture spirit through thanks.

Creating the Foundation for Spirit

Another challenge you will face in your role as leader is to be aware of, coordinate and incorporate some of each of your team member's interests into the organizational consciousness that makes decisions and sets priority-based goals. In other words, to create a sense of team spirit, the members of your team have to believe that who they are, what they do and what they mean to each other and the organization MATTERS. One of the first staff development exercises I would conduct with any new staff that I was working with was to have them identify their current life priorities, their core leadership values and what was going to make their experience on this staff matter. Each member of the staff would have an opportunity to share their information and the other members could ask questions to clarify. This simple exercise created a valuable data base of sources of mattering for our staff. Every 3 months we would revisit the exercise and adjust accordingly. This also helped in times of staff conflict when someone or something would not seem in alignment with the stated information. Don't assume your staff knows what matters to each other. Intentionally coordinate the process for them to share the information.

Challenge members to bring their best and brightest ideas to the table to make the organization matter as well. Whether it is an usher offering an idea for an improved seating plan, a co-worker suggesting a more enjoyable method for plowing through mundane paper work, or students creating options for a food drive, the encouragement and acceptance of new approaches is essential for building spirit.

By adopting and incorporating the views of your members, you as a leader demonstrate that you value the exchange of ideas, connections and open-mindedness essential to the development of a genuine community. When, at our meetings, I publicly acknowledged the ideas and strategies contributed by individual members of my head usher staff, I knew I had contributed to the creation of team spirit. I was fulfilling my role as leader. Recognition of organizational achievements through individual thanks, incentives and rewards is a very powerful way to engender spirit. Think of it as buying a thoughtful gift for someone. You really can't do it if you don't know what matters to them! Make the time to find out your member's sources of mattering and, whenever possible, align incentives with those sources!

Engendering Spirit One Person at a Time

No matter what type of organization you belong to, the potential for spirit exists. The degree to which it will develop depends upon the individuals who make up the team and their willingness to create spirit. As a team leader, your challenge is to empower each member's vision of what the team can accomplish and encourage the team spirit necessary to realize that vision.

It should be clear by now that what you do—and don't do—to foster a team spirit will be directly proportional to the productivity of your working environment. The true embodiment of spirit has to come from you. As a leader, you must transform your passions into personal visions that can fuel the spirit of the members of your team. Once they are energized, dedicated to the progress of your team, their collective passions begin to nourish the process of creating a vision for the entire organization.

Before becoming a professional speaker, I worked at a small private college in Rhode Island. I was asked to serve as a member of a team facilitating a week-long summer conference focused on the understanding and appreciation of diversity on campus. At one point a troupe of student actors presented "Oppression Theater," short skits and role plays based on actual incidents from college life. After they performed these skits for us, they remained in character for a question-and-answer period with the audience.

I found myself totally engaged in the process of asking questions and reflecting on the insights shared by others in the room. I had long been searching for a presentation format that might have just such an impact on my own campus. After the conference, I returned to Rhode Island College and tried to imagine how we might incorporate such a program ourselves.

In my role as leader, I started by analyzing what I wanted the program to accomplish. In other words, I envisioned a "finish line" for the project. Many times before I had used this mental exercise in my personal life, imagining myself owning the restaurant where I worked as a dishwasher, or visualizing myself in smaller-sized clothing as I began a new diet. Starting with the end in mind helped me to strategize my plan and set my goals. This approach—or strategy—is one that encourages your team to invest in the prioritization of goals for their organization. The exercise described below, "The Finish Line," uses creativity, innovation and FUN to engender a team vision.

The Finish Line Exercise

First, challenge your team members to imagine a finish line that represents a finite period of time, the end of the first fiscal quarter, perhaps, or the end of the first semester. Then ask them to think about what they specifically want to accomplish at the end of that time period. If you were at the end of the first quarter, you might ask, what would our team be celebrating?

Once your team has a mental image of their ideal finish line, divide them into small groups of three to five and provide them with large sheets of newsprint or banner paper and some craft supplies—markers, paints, crayons, stickers, stencils, etc. Direct them to create a drawing, sculpture, collage or any other expression of their vision. You can provide them with the following key questions to make sure there is consistent information included in each conceptualization of the finish line:

- WHO is in the picture? What is your vision of the roles the team members will play?
- WHERE are the resources necessary for the team to be successful?
- WHERE are the organizational and personal obstacles for the team?
- WHEN do you believe these goals can be achieved?
- WHO will you be thanking?
- WHY would others invest their time and energy in the goal?

Leadership in Action

To demonstrate in more detail how *The Finish Line* model can work for your organization, I'll draw again from one of my previous experiences. Specifically, in my campaign to launch an *Oppression Theater* project on my own campus, I began by sketching out some initial ideas—in the form of pictures, symbols and words—on a large sheet of paper to illustrate what I really wanted the project to accomplish. I included some key allies in students and staff members who had been supportive of my previous efforts, and added some of the scripts and other materials that I had brought back from the conference. As I worked, I realized this was going to be a very risky undertaking. It involved telling some hard truths about life on our campus, truths which administrators usually prefer not to highlight. I sketched in the obstacles presented by administrative policies and prevailing attitudes. I also included, as a positive, the energy that would no doubt infuse the audiences who were going to witness and participate in this production; I truly believed we would be able to recreate on our own campus the experience of the summer conference I had attended.

My blueprint in place, I set about to invest others in the vision. I began to recruit students and staff members by holding an organizational meeting to show them what I envisioned for the project and inviting those present to contribute their own vision. When they showed enthusiasm, I challenged them to come up with some scripts for the program. This was where the passion started to flow. I had no idea that our students faced such intense issues. They generated some amazing scripts. One in particular, on acquaintance rape, was so moving and powerful we knew immediately that we wanted to present it to the student body at large.

Now that the project was off the ground, it needed a name. In my office hung a poster with the quote, "The difference between a flower and a weed is a judgment." Once again, my friends the dandelions returned from left field. The members of our group shared my conviction that the dandelion served as an appropriate symbol for our efforts to educate about prejudice. *Dandelion Theater* was born.

With a clear vision of the finish line for *Dandelion Theater*, the next step was to bring the project to life, transforming vision into action. Specifically, we had to define priority-based goals for the group, first by facing reality. Serious incidents of exclusion and discrimination had occurred on our campus. In the past, the process of dealing with them had been to report them, document them, address them and move on. Now, through the instrument of the theater project, we hoped to learn from these challenging and sometimes embarrassing incidents, analyzing them without resorting to fault finding.

Point #5: Leaders challenge members to invest in spirit by encouraging feedback, engaging in open and honest dialogue and incorporating the resulting ideas into the policies and practices of the organization.

Eliminating the unwritten rule against closely examining issues of bias and exclusion made room for the innovative practice of using theater as a method for creatively addressing bias-based issues; at the same time, we hoped to educate ourselves about the concepts of campus community. You will need to examine, as we did, if there are members on your team that experience a feeling of exclusion or bias directly from you or other members, or from the structure and practices of your organization. This will not be an easy task, but it is imperative if you take your role as a leader seriously. Removing obsolete and unnecessary obstacles is a required practice for leaders who want to make space for the new ideas and energy generated from the group.

Maintaining Your Team Spirit

Do you matter? If you reflect upon your experience with any group with which you have maintained a lasting connection, you will no doubt realize that your fellow members—be they friends, co-workers or family—made you feel as though you mattered. They cultivated a spirit of belonging, purpose and value in you as well as in each of your associates. In effect, your worth to the group was in direct correlation to the group's worth to you.

We have a tremendous capacity to instill this spirit of mattering into our collective consciousness, as proven in particular by the events of September 11, 2001 in New York City and Washington D.C. The swell of patriotic spirit and the outpouring of concern, with a genuine need and willingness to help, had not been seen in this country in decades. We have seen what we are capable of and, as a result, have raised the bar of what we can and should expect from one another. Our leaders have demonstrated their ability to put aside differences when priorities shift and the focus needs to be on the common good.

> "No pessimist ever discovered the secret of the stars,
> or sailed to an un-chartered land,
> or opened a new doorway for the human spirit."
> – Helen Keller

The challenge before us now is to maintain that positive outlook and nurture our spirit. Without losing sight of the lessons learned from past experience, we must cultivate the sources of inspiration and mattering that will prepare us for an ever-changing and dynamic future. As a leader, your attitude must be one like of the optimist.

I don't believe that a pessimist could have hit that homerun back when I was in fifth grade. I thank Mark Davis for being a leader who gave me one of my first tastes of mattering. Since then, my own life has been filled with examples of why spirit-centered leadership can change not only organizations, but individual lives. The applause that erupted on the opening night of *Dandelion Theater* showed our troupe that a collaborative and cooperative team spirit can turn dreams into a reality that makes a difference for many others—that our efforts MATTERED.

In a world where individual effort rarely seems to count, the leaders of the organizations that make up our collective community need to embrace the power of spirit, creating an environment where their members want to be viable, mattering parts of the team.

That's the stuff softballs and dandelions are made of.

CHAPTER SUMMARY

❑ A leader is responsible for modeling and engendering a positive spirit in their organization.

❑ Interpersonal communication is the lifeblood of spirit.

❑ Leaders empower members to empathically understand, appreciate and celebrate the diversity of all members as a foundation for an authentic and valuing organization.

❑ Leaders make intentional efforts to nurture spirit through thanks.

❑ Leaders challenge members to invest in spirit by encouraging feedback, engaging in open and honest dialogue and incorporating the resulting ideas into the policies and practices of the organization.

4

On Strategic Planning
The Voice of Rick Barnes

*"If you don't know where you're going,
you might end up somewhere else."*
    — Yogi Berra

In any organization, a strategic plan is the basis for strong governance, effective leadership and sound management. It provides direction for the effective operation of the organization as a whole. The initiation of the plan often arouses interest and enthusiasm, serving as a catalyst for renewed purpose among the leadership and members of the group alike. By engendering pride in the deliberate and rational performance of the organization, a strategic plan unifies members in their commitment to a common vision and goals.

Without a vision, the future of any organization remains uncertain. Vision is closely tied to the establishment of a mission, which in turn provides direction for the plan for the future, a strategic plan for the continued development of the organization. Unfortunately, too many organizations avoid strategic planning, citing excuses ranging from lack of organizational time to the costs required for hiring consultants; moreover, when things are going well, leaders question the need for planning at all. Why fix what's not broken?

*"The task of the leader is to get his/her people
from where they are to where they have not been."*
    — Henry Kissinger

Getting others to where they need to be is next to impossible without a plan of action. Strategic planning is one of the most powerful tools an organization can use to advance itself to the next level, to put forth a common purpose, and to fulfill the goals of its membership. In order to maintain the interest of the participants, a plan must offer opportunities for rapid, visible progress. It is critical to align all of the components of the organization in order to achieve the objectives laid out in the strategic plan. The plan answers much more than simply, "What are we going to do?" It also answers "How?" and "Why?" A strategic plan is literally the key to the future of the organization.

Developing an Effective Tool that Works

Effective leaders, no matter what type of organization they work for, are able to identify problems, plan ahead and anticipate results. Most important, they need to understand how to implement a strong strategic plan by setting direction and priorities. Leaders depend upon a plan to serve as the "syllabus" for the organization, using it to establish the minimum expectations for progress, institute deadlines for the attainment of goals, and project the desired outcome.

We all depend on planning in our daily lives. Have you ever tried to embark upon a weight loss plan? First you try to decide whether you need to lose weight, envisioning how different you might look, or how much better you might feel, five or ten or even twenty pounds lighter. Perhaps you think about it privately; maybe you talk it over with a good friend, a spouse, a parent or a colleague. Once your vision leads to a goal (i.e. I'm going to lose fifteen pounds by Thanksgiving), you set about to plot out a plan of action. You establish a series of objectives in support of your goal. You begin to watch what you eat, start a program of regular exercise, and figure out how to achieve more balance in your life. You might turn to others for assistance as you develop your plan (a published diet plan, your family doctor), and continue to ask for their support as the weeks go by and you get closer to meeting your goal.

Once you begin your campaign to lose weight, you don't set your plan aside. Instead, you refer to it regularly, keeping track of what you eat and weighing yourself regularly to see how many pounds you are losing, always with one eye on your final goal. You may turn to those around you for input and direction, visiting your doctor to make sure your body is responding well to its new regimen or a dietitian to help you choose the right foods for a healthy lifestyle. A fitness specialist might give you advice about the best form of exercise for your body and how to adjust your workouts as you become more fit. Each of these consultants provides direction according to the ultimate goal that you have set for yourself in your weight loss plan.

Finally, as Thanksgiving approaches, you step on the scale and discover you have lost those fifteen pounds. You applaud your progress and so do those around you. Thanks to the successful completion of your plan, you are healthier, stronger and more committed to a wholesome way of living. As the leader of your own personal organization, you have helped to initiate, continue and achieve the vision promulgated by your strategic plan. And now you work to maintain your desired weight, continuing to watch what you eat, evaluating your continued commitment to the plan, etc.

STEPS TOWARD A STRATEGIC PLAN

There are seven specific steps involved in strategic planning which include the following:

Step I. Vision	*Step V. Strategies*
Step II. Mission	*Step VI. Activation*
Step III. Plans for Planning	*Step VII. Evaluation*
Step IV. Goals/Objectives	

Step I. The Vision

The development of a *vision* is the initial stage in the strategic planning process. Imagine your organization five, ten, fifteen years from now. What do you see? As you lead this brainstorming session with the members of your group, try to discover the dreams you have in common. Our hopes and dreams pull us into the future. This vision of the ideal future is the foundation of your strategic plan, the first tentative step toward fundamental change. Without a concrete vision, it is impossible to move forward in the process of planning. The members of any organization have to be able to envision the end result; a vision provides a clear picture of the goals they are trying to achieve—together. It is important that your members can see their own dreams encapsulated in the vision for the organization; if they believe their personal goals are a critical part of the overall purpose, you can count on them to get involved and stay involved. Vision is much more than "what ought to be." It represents specific aspirations in which members believe deeply, their very personal desires for the future. Do not underestimate the importance of this process; establishing a vision provides an outcome-oriented endpoint around which the entire organization can rally.

Helpful Tips for Visioning:

- Consider, exactly what difference is it that you and your organization want to make.

- Clarify problem areas rather than exploit them.

- The vision must come from the heart—specific aspirations in which members deeply believe.

- Organize various visions into common themes—leads toward overall areas to focus on when writing the actual strategic plan.

- Do not get mixed up between the desire simply to do something rather than doing something good.

Step II. The Mission

If you are struggling to identify a purpose for your group, imagine what things might be like if you didn't exist. What would be missing in your community, your industry or your profession? What special contributions do you make? The answers to these questions will help reveal the ideal purpose, or *mission* of your organization. Mission defines "why" behind the "what" it is that you are here to do. It is an overall guide for direction, establishing the basic justification for the organization's existence.

Mission can often be expressed in brief statements. Think of some of the slogans you've seen on television or in print advertising: "The Ultimate Driving Machine," "Nothing Runs Like a Deere," or "We Love to Fly, and It Shows." These mission statements, all very public statements of intent and desire, reveal the fundamental mission of each of these major companies. In their effort to create a public image, they also provide direction for all those within the organization who accept responsibility for its success. A powerful mission statement should include six critical components which are presented below.

Mission Statements

1. Mission statements should always utilize results terminology.

The difference between results and consequences is that results are what you expect while consequences are what you get. Therefore, it could be safe to expect that if your expectations are positive, your results will be as well. Your mission statement should express what you expect. It should state the results you expect from your actions, from the things your organization does.

2. Mission statements should be succinct in presentation, using few words and sentences.

The Mission is the guide—it's not the act itself. It provides direction, it is the core for all you do, it is the synthesis of how your organization is seen. It should be brief. It should be written in such a way that is easily remembered and understood. Short enough to put on a card in every office. Brief enough that it can be stated clearly by every member or employee.

3. **Mission statements should use authoritative generation, making sure to involve all members in the process of mission development.**

The development of the Mission should involve all members of your organization. The members, in fact, will be expected to use it as their guide. The old adage, you tend to support the things you help to create, stands true for the mission of your organization. The various constituencies should be utilized through open opportunities to provide direction to the Mission Statement.

4. **Mission statements should use vertical generation, connecting the leadership to the general membership of the organization.**

It is the job of the leader to see that planning takes place and that it is done well. It is also important that the leaders actively participate in the process. However, the statement should also include active involvement from the entire membership. As a result of equal participation from all levels of the organization, the Mission serves as an appropriate statement for the organization as a whole.

5. **Mission statements should use horizontal generation, encouraging ownership of the mission at all levels within the group.**

As in item number four, the development of the mission should come from all members of the organization. Ownership of the mission statement must also come from all levels. Again, one tends to support the things one helps to create. For the mission statement to serve in the most effective manner it must be held by all members of the group.

6. **The mission it promulgates should be pervasive, visible everywhere within the organization.**

On the wall in the board room, at the top of meeting agenda's, on the cover of staff handbooks, everywhere you look, the mission must be visible and readily understood by the members of the organization. It should permeate all levels, from the top leader to the newest member. The mission should guide all decisions of the organization.

The mission, honestly, provides direction for the overall operation of the group as a whole.

Tips for Writing a Mission:

- Involve all levels of the organization in the process.
- Short and simple is always better than long and confusing.
- Reflects the major values of the organization.
- The mission defines the "why" behind "what" you do.

Step III. "Plans" for Planning

After you have established the parameters of your vision and produced your mission statement, you must prepare for the initiation of your *plan*. Measure the existing strengths and weaknesses of your organization—to establish a baseline, if you will. Where are you today in comparison to where you want to be in the future? How are you doing in terms of finances, personnel, resources, technology, attitudes, commitments and so forth? What are your growth trends, leadership changes, policy trends? What are your external opportunities and threats, including demographic, political, economic and technological trends? What are the national, regional, state and local trends? You must make the time and effort to educate your members about outside influences and surrounding issues that affect the health and future of your organization. What are the things around you that might create or restrict opportunities for change?

Review your responses first, narrowing to the choices that will be readily available to you. At this early point in the planning process, any option can be considered a good one. The diversity of your group should engender multiple answers to questions about the appropriate direction for the organization, based on your common vision. As these options are narrowed in the course of discussion, they will lead naturally to the adoption of choices appropriate to the specific desires of your group. The planning process always focuses on implementation, asking not only "why?" but "how?" If one of the goals for the organization is to expand the membership, you must ask "how?" If the answer is to begin a membership drive, you must ask "how?" If the answer is to develop a plan of action, you must ask "how?" If the answer is to appoint a membership committee, you must ask "how?" This ongoing process of question and answer leads, very simply, to a step-by-step plan toward the ultimate fulfillment of the goal—in this case, membership growth.

Tips for Planning for the Strategic Plan:

- It is important to determine where you currently are in comparison to where you want to be.

- In processing through planning, ask not only "why" but "how?"

- The notes from the planning stage will lead directly to the written Strategic Plan.

Step IV. The "Meat" of the Plan— Goals and Objectives

"You have to know where you are going,
be able to state it clearly and concisely—
and you have to care about it passionately."

– Tom Peters

Assuming you have successfully defined a vision for your organization and you understand your mission, you have reached the point in the strategic planning process where you must develop a series of *goals and objectives* that will lead you toward the fulfillment of that vision.

Goals, and their related objectives, are major strategic intentions that will lead your organization into the future. Your goals relate directly to your mission statement. Although they are specific statements of intent, goals also highlight broad areas of responsibility consistent with the mission of the organization. In setting goals, you should limit yourself, selecting no more than five to ten at a time. Anything beyond that number and you will become bogged down with specific details of the organization. These details are the work of the membership in fulfilling the ultimate goals and the organization.

Your goals and objectives should be precise, measurable, result-oriented statements of progress. In other words, goals specify what needs to be achieved within a given period of time as you work to realize the overall strategic plan. Resist the temptation to dream up lofty statements. The members of your group should prioritize goals, determining which are of most immediate importance. The lower the priority, the longer you have to achieve them. However, do not eliminate those goals that at first seem less pressing. As you review your plan on a regular basis, you will most likely need to adjust your goals according to ongoing progress and development within the organization. A less important goal today may become your first priority tomorrow.

Tips for Goals and Objectives:

- A few specific goals are always better than lots of general statements.

- Goals should always be measurable.

- Do not set a goal too tough OR too easy—achieving a goal is a positive experience, which encourages you to achieve more goals. While goals should challenge, they should also be attainable.

- Make sure your short-range goals are consistent with your long-range goals.

- Goals should always be stated positively rather than negatively.

Step V. Developing Action Strategies

The establishment of goals and objectives will almost certainly lead to a call for specific changes within your organization. One of the first areas for review may be personnel. You may discover a need for additional staff or volunteer leaders. A change in leadership, both in terms of specific roles and individual commitment, may be necessary for the organization to institute positive changes. By setting the right direction and appropriate priorities, you will be able to empower the membership as you assign responsibility for specific parts of the plan.

It is likely that a review of your budget will be necessary. The planned use of resources should reflect support for the strategic plan. Some *strategies for action* may also call for fundamental changes in the organization's rules and regulations, or even the bylaws, while others may require only revised committee appointments or adjusted volunteer commitments within the group. All components of the organization must be reviewed to ensure they are aligned in such a manner that will serve to achieve the goals and objectives outlined by the plan. The period of transition and transformation that may follow is important, but it should not delay the progress of the group. It may simply be an opportunity to shift gears from what was to what is yet to be.

Tips for Action:

- Let your goals run your organization—if the goals require changes (personnel, leadership, etc.), then make the appropriate change.

- Let your goals run your budget—if the goal was important enough, don't let it die for lack of resources.

- Make sure your rules/regulations are compatible with the goals of your organization.

Step VI. Activation of the Plan

In initiating your organization's commitment to its new strategic plan, you might want to kick off the process with a public announcement and an official celebration. This will offer an opportunity for you to formally reflect on the past, reviewing the steps that have taken you this far, to thank those who have played critical roles in your success, and to recognize your progress to date. Such a public observance signals a point of departure from the past and a step into the future for your organization. It will allow you to share the plan with others, as you make an official acknowledgment to your supporters and shareholders. You will be able to rally your members as you each take that step forward in formal commitment to the new direction outlined by your strategic plan.

Tips for Activating the Plan:

- Look for the best way to kick off your new plan (public statement, organization rally, etc.).

- Make sure the new plan is shared widely and that those within the organization can explain and defend its statements.

- This is a point of new beginning—recognize it as such.

Step VII. Ongoing Evaluation

It is critical that you develop a reliable system for assessing, monitoring and *evaluating* the progress of the strategic plan. While evaluation may remain the primary responsibility of the leadership, or executive board, you may also find it necessary to formalize the assessment process by appointing a specific committee of members. A single member should be assigned to lead this process, charged to report regularly to the membership about how successful the organization has been at remaining "on plan." If it is diligent in its duties, the members of this committee may very well be the first in your organization to recognize the need to revise the plan itself or to suggest adjustments that will better meet the stated goals and objectives.

Tips for Evaluation:

- Evaluate, evaluate, evaluate—measure all you do against the purpose for doing it.

- Measure—if you were successful, how successful; if you need more work, how much more work.

- Document—be the best you can be, but utilize your evaluation to help the next group be even better. Ongoing progress and development is the ultimate goal.

Review of Strategic Planning

Step I. Vision – what do we want to be?

Step II. Mission – the reason for being.

Step III. Plans for Planning – costs/assets/facilities/staff, etc.

Step IV. Goals/Objectives – statements of measurable results.

Step V. Strategies – how to reach objectives.

Step VI. Activation – initiate the plan.

Step VII. Evaluation – review and revise.

> *"Meticulous planning will enable everything*
> *you do to appear spontaneous."*
> *– Mark Caine*

Ongoing Process

Change is, of course, at the heart of strategic planning, yet the essence of good planning lies in balancing necessary changes and high standards of continuity. As you move forward in your strategic planning process, you will continue to have the opportunity to reflect upon those things you do well. By encouraging the strengths of your organization and implementing new ways to make it even better, the plan will lead you toward continual progress and development.

It is important to link all items on your organization's agenda to the strategic plan. You will find that small, incremental steps will take you far toward the fulfillment of the plan. The challenge before the group is to recognize that the strategic planning process, once set in motion, is a permanent guide that provides clear direction and purpose for the organization. As the plan is formally reviewed on a regular basis, it will lead to new visions, new thoughts, new ideas, new goals, new objectives. You should consistently require staff and volunteers to report on key accomplishments in the context of the plan. Moreover, the leadership itself must be prepared to recommend revisions in the overall process.

A common commitment to pursuing a shared vision through ongoing strategic planning is the key to the continued progress and development of your organization. A strategic plan, implemented correctly, can reenergize the membership and create a more enjoyable and successful organization. It all begins with a dream—a vision for the future. Vision leads to a plan of action, utilizing goals and objectives. The plan that results produces positive change and a dedication to progress, serving as a catalyst for the renewed vitality of the leadership in its ongoing direction of the group. The Strategic Plan ensures a commitment to a common vision and a common purpose, vital for the effective operation of any organization.

> *"If you can dream it, you can achieve it."*
> – Walt Disney

CHAPTER SUMMARY

❑ Strategic planning is the basis for effective leadership.

❑ The anticipation of potential problems is part of the planning process.

❑ Six specific steps allow the leader to initiate, direct and achieve the group's vision.

❑ Personal objectives can also be achieve through strategic planning.

❑ Mission statements direct the leader's energies.

5

On the Soul of Leadership
The Voice of Kathy Humphrey

The soul is the Intellect, Will and the Emotion.
If my left side is pinned down and unable to move,
my soul is still free
for it cannot be pinned down unless I shut it down.
If my right side is paralyzed because of some
medical condition, if I have the energy to search
deep within myself, I will find that all pieces
of my soul are still operating.
If others try to block my vision,
to blind me to things that are going on around me,
my soul will see in spite of their efforts
for my soul looks past
what my eyes can see.

Soul has nothing to do with the color of your skin, nor the rhythmic way in which you can move your body. Soul has nothing to do with cornbread, fried chicken, macaroni and cheese, or collard greens. The soul is that which makes us who we really are, leading us to make fundamental connections with our fellow men and women. All great leaders have the ability to connect; these vital human connections supersede our physical realities.

When I hear the word "leadership," I immediately think about the strong leaders who have played major roles in my life. These people, many of them mentors, helped to make me into the leader that I am today and that I am striving to be tomorrow. It was not their positions that helped me and others to recognize them as leaders. It was not their style, physical appearance or popularity that convinced me they were leaders. It wasn't even their words. No, what I saw came from within: from their souls. For you see, their souls clearly articulated messages that would build strong leaders, and those leaders were able not only to complete tasks both large and small but more importantly to work to make a difference in the lives of others.

There are many effective definitions of leadership. In their book, Susan Komives, Nance Lucas, and Timothy McMahon (Exploring Leadership, 1998) explain that leadership is an attempt to accomplish or change something; it is a relationship founded in trust and confidence. James M. Kouzes and Barry Z. Posner (The Leadership Challenge, 1987) maintain that leadership is a dialogue, not a monologue; according to Robert K. Greenleaf (On Becoming a Servant-Leader, 1996) leadership is the ability to serve others until they are ready to serve themselves. To some extent, I agree with all of these definitions of leadership. Yet I believe that only the leader who leads with soul can truly know who s/he is, understand what s/he must become, and be willing to do something that will make a difference in our world.

> *"To thine own self be true."*
> *– Shakespeare*

Know Yourself

Whenever I interview someone who will serve as a leader on my team, I always ask, "who are you?" Often, I am met with a puzzled response or an attempt to stall such as, "Wow, that is a good question." I don't ask the question in order to stump the candidate; rather, I ask it because I want to know the person behind the list of skills and accomplishments on the resume. If you don't know who you are, I can't teach you, and I can't afford to place my responsibilities in your hands.

A leader must know who he or she is, and why he or she is the leader. If you are expending energy to make sure that other people know that you are the leader, you are not leading; you are simply attempting to be the leader. Play along with me for a while. Now, take a look at the clock and give yourself three minutes to come up with 15 phenomenal things about yourself. Okay, finished? How hard was it? For many of you, it was probably quite difficult. Our society does a terrific job of helping us to remember the negative things about ourselves, but not much to help us create a positive belief system.

Every leader faces storms, for they blow away the unnecessary and provide opportunities for new growth. Joyce Meyer [Joyce Meyer Ministries] uses the illustration of an oak tree to symbolize a strong person. If a strong person can be represented by an oak, then a strong leader requires the strength of a sequoia. A sequoia, with its ancient root system, is virtually unshakable; it would take a mighty wind, a powerful storm, or a tremendous earthquake to make it fall. If a leader builds a comparable personal foundation, the strong winds of adversity and the rains of discontent will find it nearly impossible to knock him or her down.

So what must you do to withstand the storms of leadership and keep your soul intact? You must build a positive belief system for yourself. Think about this: if you dwell only on your negative characteristics, won't it be easy to agree when someone comes along and puts you down? If you don't have the elasticity of the sequoia tree, you will add the unfavorable opinions of others to your own list of personal negatives and therefore make yourself even weaker. You can and you must be the one to determine how others view you. It all begins with you.

I challenge you once again to think seriously about your dynamic, positive qualities. Take a moment to make a list of them and post it where you will see it every day. This list will serve as a reminder to you that you are an awesome person with awesome gifts and abilities. You must create a CD that runs only in your head and it must be entitled "The Good Things I Know About Me." If you take the time daily to remind yourself about your good qualities, you will have the power and energy to fix the things about you that need work. You will be able to keep your weaker attributes in perspective. A positive belief system must be worked on every day, for there is always someone waiting to undermine you. With your system firmly in place, they may be able to shake you but they won't tear you down. You will be able to stand fast, reaching toward the sky to achieve your dreams.

Every day before I leave for work, I look in the mirror and give myself the first smile of the day. I may be having a bad hair day, but I smile; my lipstick may not match my outfit perfectly, but I smile; my children may be screaming in the background because one has looked at the other one the wrong way, but I smile; I may have the biggest white zit in the middle of my African-American forehead, but I find something that I like about myself. I smile and remind myself that no one on this earth put the smile on my face and no one is going to take it away. I tell myself that I am confident and competent, and just before I turn off the bathroom light, I look in the mirror and I say, "You go, girl!" Knowing who you are will give you the guts to stand up for what you believe is good and right.

It is not enough for you to tell others what you value;
you must show them.

Know Your Own Values

It is only when I see you standing up for what you believe in that I truly understand you. Remember the wisdom of the statements, "If you don't stand for something, you will fall for anything," and "Actions speak louder than words: if your words don't match your actions, no one will trust you; if they don't trust you, they cannot follow you."

Every now and then, I catch myself being inconsistent, my actions contradicting my words. Whenever this happens, I challenge myself either to reevaluate my values or do a better job of living up to who I say I am. If I claim to value all people, then I must ask myself why I do not treat all who cross my path with the same respect. Position, economic status, body type, age or sexuality should not matter. If I say that I love everyone, then that love must have no end and no beginning.

With my value structure intact, I am better able to manage the emotional roller coaster that we all must ride in this life. No one is going to follow someone who is always flying off the handle or always depressed. Why should I go with you when you haven't learned how to lead yourself? In order to be able to give of yourself as a leader, you have to refresh and renew yourself constantly. Only you know how to provide yourself with what you need. Many of those around you may be singing "What Have You Done For Me Lately?" but unless you learn to do for yourself, you will not become a leader who leads with soul; others will feed off you until your soul dissipates and there is nothing left.

Laughter is the best medicine I know. When I was a child, my father would laugh so hard that at times he would fall to the floor and roll. Of course I, too, laughed and fell to the floor with him. To this day, I make sure that laughter is a part of my life every single day. Laughter naturally renews the body, providing stress relief. Surround yourself with people you enjoy and who enjoy you.

With your emotions under control, you will respect yourself; self-respect, in turn, will make it easy for you to respect others and their opinions. Expect others to disagree with you and it won't rattle you as much. Remember that some people like to be contrary just for the heck of it. Ever meet someone who is never satisfied? Don't try to satisfy them; it is not your responsibility to make sure everyone is happy all the time. Learn to recognize the type of person who annoys you and make sure that you give him or her the same respect you give to anyone else.

One day, I was sitting in a meeting with a man who always gets under my skin. He and I do not share the same value system and so it is easy for me to let him bother me. Every time he spoke, I knew he was irritating the leader as much he was me. I wanted to scream, "Will you shut up!" But the leader in that group was patient, continually giving him opportunities to speak. She showed him respect. When I thought hard about it, I realized that this man who annoys me from time to time really had some good ideas. Don't allow your organization to miss out on opportunities because your emotions make it hard for you to recognize it when great ideas come in unattractive packages.

"A leader with courage and an iron will
is unstoppable and unbeatable."

— David Blunt

Being the Leader

In your search for the soul of your leadership, remember that confidence and self-awareness are essential for good leadership, but it is even more important to master the art of being the leader. Think about the first time you got excited about being the leader. When my boys started kindergarten a few years ago, I had an opportunity to remember that being the leader first became famous in kindergarten. The boys soon discovered the joys and the stresses of becoming the line leader. Being the leader was a special thing, wasn't it? You got to do everything first! My boys enjoyed it so much that they wanted us to walk around the house in a line so they could take turns being the leader. When we were driving, they would say "Mama, Mama, get in front of that car so that we can be the leader!"

But being the leader also means that I have to be fair and consistent. Being the leader means that I have a greater responsibility because I can see better at the head of the line. The people behind me are depending on me to do my work with integrity. They depend upon me to see more and they depend upon me to be more.

Being the leader means I cannot be afraid to take risks. I once heard that failure is only a dress rehearsal for success. If you allow the possibility of failure to hold you hostage then you will never accomplish anything significant. You will become a maintainer. Nothing great has ever come from one who was unwilling to take risks. As a leader, you must be excited about the opportunities to bring about positive change; that change will come only if you make a decision to move forward, even when you know that the road ahead will not be smooth.

Have you ever sat through a meeting where absolutely nothing was accomplished because no one was willing to make a decision? Why won't they make decisions? They don't want to assume responsibility. In a social setting, when you are asked which restaurant or movie you would like to go to and you say, "I don't care," you are refusing to own the responsibility for the evening; if things don't turn out well, then it's no skin off your back.

> "Great things happen only when someone
> is willing to visualize, internalize and verbalize
> a better way of doing something."
> – Dr. Ira B. Hilliard
> New Light Christian Center Church

Being the leader is crucial, but you can't be the leader if you will not step forward to make a positive difference. You can't accomplish anything without taking time to reflect on a better tomorrow. But you must be able to do more than just see it; you also have to believe that you can do it, that you can, in effect, make the impossible possible. If you don't believe it can happen, it can't. It you don't think it can work, it won't. There is no way in the world that you will be able to motivate someone else to work toward a goal that you yourself don't believe in or that you think is too difficult to tackle.

If you are willing to do more than dream, you can make your dream a reality. If you can tell others about your dream in a way that excites them, they will see the benefit of becoming part of it themselves; the dream then becomes their dream, too, a common goal for everyone associated with your team. But they cannot be motivated unless you draw them in, unless they can see and feel the dream that has been born in the depths of your soul. For when the mouth speaks with the voice of the soul, it is much more convincing.

The soul, by drawing vivid, clear pictures, can break your dream down into small digestible pieces that will inspire others to work to bring it to life. And the soul will keep you mindful that you, as a leader, are merely a servant to all of those who have adopted your dream as theirs. The soul will shield you even when others try to steal the accolades and applause; it is not always important to be recognized as the dreamer if the world has become a better place to live in. Rather than focusing on external rewards, the leader who leads with soul is much more concerned about honoring those who helped to fulfill the dream.

The soul of a leader is in the Knowing, Being and Doing. It is the soul of the leader that moves the team forward, and enables the leader to climb even when others doubt their abilities.

You Know Me When You See Me, For I Am the Soul of Leadership

I am flexible and never static.
I am ethical, principled and sure of my values.
My integrity is easy to see, and I believe you know me when you see me.
I am respectful and I have the ability to see things from your perspective.
Your differences do not alarm me or cause me
to doubt myself or my abilities.
I am sure that you know me when you see me.
I am powerful, for I believe in my abilities
to make the world more dynamic.
I believe in my abilities to motivate you and others so that you can see
the greatness that you and I can develop together.
I am sure that you know me when you see me.
I am committed to every task I take on, and I can see
the sun shining on a cloudy day.
I can see peace in the midst of a storm.
I will climb the mountain even though
everyone else says it cannot be done.
You know you know me when you see me.
You know me, for when I am not present people tend to complain
about my absences, for I, I am the soul of leadership.
You know me, for when you don't see me,
apathy and detachment reign supreme,
but with me you are powerful.

You know me, for I have roots within your being,
that can only grow if you believe in me, use me, try me.
I am the soul of leadership,
and if you use me, you can be great,
for I, for I, I am you.

CHAPTER SUMMARY

❑ You are not really leading until your entire being (the soul) is involved.

❑ Every talent, every gift that you possess are your special tools, that you have been given to lead with your soul.

❑ Every leader is driven by possibilities that appear to be opportunities to make something great occur.

❑ If a leader is not comfortable with who they have been created to be, they will not have the fortitude to manage the storms of leadership.

6

On Creativity

The Voice of Lenny Dave

Be persistent. Take action on your ideas.
And don't let those negative people get you down!

What drives me nuts? Giving up before you even get started! All too often, you'll hear someone in an organization respond to a suggestion for change with the phrase, "But we've always done it this way!" Even worse is the default confession, "Oh, I'm not really a creative person." These statements may be expressed in genuine innocence, or as a bold proclamation of premature creative surrender.

Both phrases are symptoms of a serious disease in the creative sick ward. Fortunately, there is a cure. You'll begin to see results after the first dose, but the greater your commitment to the medicine, the exponentially greater will be your personal and organizational return.

Human beings were born with the divinely inspired ability to bring new thoughts and ideas into the world. Stop and think for a moment about that all-encompassing statement. The more I read, write and live the awesome gift of our personal creativity and the amazing capabilities of the human mind, the more I keep coming back to a handful of fundamental concepts. No matter what your title or job description, you can use these concepts to nurture your creative thinking ability and apply it in the workplace, in the community and in your personal life.

The Value of Creativity

New ideas translate directly to the bottom line. What's a new idea worth to your organization? Maybe it's an idea that helps the flow of information, either digitally, on paper or in human interaction. Perhaps it's an idea that helps to retain valuable employees while attracting talented new ones. It might be an idea that helps to bring in a new client or, for that matter, keep an existing account from walking across the street to your competition. Or, maybe it's just an idea that will, to the delight of your shareholders, ultimately increase the value of your company's stock. What would you pay for a single idea that did any of the above? Below are ten fundamental concepts for building your creative talents.

Creativity is the ability to generate,
express and implement new ideas.

THE CONCEPTS OF CREATIVITY

#1 Creativity Concept: Creative Leadership is Action-Oriented

If you wait for everything to be absolutely perfect before you act to implement an idea, you'll be covered in cobwebs as the world passes you by. Creative leadership is about moving organizations forward. On a personal level, it's about moving yourself forward. Yes, creative leadership involves helping the people around you to express their ideas. But more than that, creative leadership means taking action on some of those ideas. And when the results bring something genuinely new and valuable to the marketplace, you have made the leap from creativity into innovation. To the extent that you as a leader are able to capitalize on those unique ideas, the greater your impact.

However, personal and organizational creativity is not something that can be mandated from upstairs in a company-wide or departmental memo: "Effective tomorrow morning at 8:00 a.m., everyone is expected to be more creative. Failure to adhere to this new policy will be duly noted and factored heavily into your next performance evaluation. Have a nice day!"

"It is a very grave mistake to think that the enjoyment
of seeing and searching can be promoted by
means of coercion and a sense of duty. "
— Albert Einstein

There must be a buy-in from the top down in order to establish
a working environment where creative energy can be cultivated and
new ideas can be brought forth from the bottom up and implemented.
Before we reveal the simplicity of the creative thinking process, let's
take a moment to examine three of the major factors that get in the
way: Negative Thinking, Fear and Risk.

#2 Creativity Concept: The World Around Us is Negative

Negative thinking and negative energy is highly toxic and
extremely contagious. It's not just what we say and do to others
and what they say and do to us. All too often, our creative thinking
ability is undermined by what we say and do to ourselves. Don't
sabotage your own success. There are leaders, as well as members,
that take great pride in perpetuating a negative self-fulfilling
prophecy: "Why should I speak up? Nobody ever listens to my ideas.
They think I'm an idiot. I'll never get that promotion. Don't expect
me to step forward next time they come looking for volunteers!
You see? What did I tell you? They're out to get me, those
backstabbers!"

It's a sad fact that it's easier to be negative and critical than it is
to be positive and constructive. As a leader, you want to set a positive, appreciative perspective on being creative. Lead by example.
Embrace creative thought and design so others will follow.

"Fear is the little dark room where
negatives are developed."
— Humorist Michael Pritchard

#3 Creativity Concept: Creative Leadership Involves Embracing Failure

Are you possibly afraid you're not a creative individual, yet you are the leader? Confront your fear. Today, there are phobias for just about everything, maybe even one for people who are afraid to read motivational self-help books on leadership! No one enjoys making mistakes, but they are an important and normal part of the learning process. Unfortunately, many people have developed a serious fear of failure and rejection. They hesitantly go about their lives and leadership positions in reluctant anticipation of perceived pain. Fear has been referred to as an acronym (actually an acrostic) standing for False Evidence (or Expectation) Appearing Real. Have you sat in the dentist's chair recently?

Fear is a natural human emotion. It is a triggered response designed to protect you from danger. In that regard, it is entirely normal to experience fear. Confident leaders successfully deal with it every day. But when your personal and organizational fears begin to inordinately affect your behavior and block the creative experience, then you have a situation on your hands. Some people repeatedly play to their fears and continually emphasize their own limitations. Being tentative or cautious doesn't have to kill an organization. It doesn't have to destroy your potential to make a difference. You will learn more from your failures than you will from your successes. Thomas Edison was once asked if it bothered him that he had failed in over 250 attempts to invent the light bulb. His response: "Not at all. In fact, I was successful in discovering 250 ways that wouldn't work!"

> *"Success is not built upon success.*
> *Success is built upon failure and adversity*
> *and how we turn it around."*
>
> *– Sumner Redstone*

Fear doesn't have to detract and distract you from action. Consider Steve Irwin, television's Crocodile Hunter on the Animal

Planet channel. Here's an otherwise normal guy who (along with his wife, no less!) genuinely rejoices in picking up poisonous snakes, chasing crocodiles and basically embracing our deadliest fears. But think for a moment. Does Steve Irwin experience fear? According to Mark Twain, "Courage is the resistance to fear and the mastery of fear—but not the absence of fear." Of course Irwin has fear. But, he has learned through knowledge and experience how to resist and master it.

#4 Creativity Concept: Creative Leadership Requires Taking Purposeful Risks

Now, I'm not suggesting you start bungee jumping off bridges or wrestle with reptiles. Rather, I'm urging you to take measured, intentional risks by trying to improve something by doing it differently or better—the purposeful risk involved in the pursuit of a creative new idea. Chances are taken, not given. By nature, we are creatures of comfort, and life in the comfort zone is good. It's time to step out of your comfort zone. Think about the thermostat in your home or office. That comfort zone is often marked in red, usually between 70-74 degrees. But nothing exciting happens in the comfort zone. There is no reason to get up off the proverbial couch. You have mastered a pattern of behavior that is now your routine. You find comfort in knowing what to expect. Well, watch what happens when the thermostat hits a stuffy 80 degrees. You respond. You move. You get up off the couch.

> *"Only those who will risk going too far can possibly find out how far one can go!"*
> – T. S. Eliot

There is a direct correlation between purposeful risk and creativity. The more purposeful risk there is involved in generating, expressing and implementing an idea, the more creative, new and different it tends to be—and vice versa.

#5 Creativity Concept: Creative Leadership Involves Searching for More Than One Right Answer

Thinking Outside of the Box

What exactly is this box that everyone always talks about? "The Box" represents self-imposed, self-perceived boundaries, barriers, limits and rules about the way you think, act and lead. Creative leaders know that change is the only constant. The way things are now is not the way they must always be. You, as a leader, can choose to be proactive and question the normal way of thinking—or continually play catch up. Either way, change will happen.

When faced with a product, process or program in need of a creative makeover, one of the best ways to think outside of the box involves the challenging exercise of asking simple questions. But the trick is not in the asking. That's the easy part. The trick is to allow yourself and those around you to begin to answer the questions without fear of criticism or judgment. Go for quantity of answers. Solicit input from all levels of your organization. Keep in mind that initial creative impulses and responses may not make sense at first.

Begin with the end. What is the goal? What is the purpose? What is the desired outcome? Next, challenge the parameters and variables which already exist. Look for new, better and different ways of doing things. But first, you must believe that those ways exist.

"Everything has been thought of before.
The problem is to think of them again."
– Goethe

Another strategy for thinking outside of the box is to avoid the temptation to influence the group's creative thinking process by issuing a pre-determined conclusion. Allow for the likelihood that more than one right answer exists. (It does.) Rather than limiting people by asking them to find the answer, ask "How many right answers can we find?"

Be confident that the people around you will find those answers. Expose them to new ways of doing things. Make the investment to teach them the fundamentals of creative thinking. Let them experience and get comfortable with the process. Then politely get out of their way. Don't let your ego interfere with good ideas that come from someone else or which you don't initially understand.

#6 Creativity Concept: Understanding the Creative Thinking Process is as Simple as 1-2-3

The Creative Process

Volume after volume has been written about the creative thinking process. Some have colorful analogies, others are filled with technical terminology, but the fundamental concepts are basically the same. So for the sake of simplicity, lets make it as easy as 1-2-3.

Step #1 is an active process that utilizes the conscious mind. With a personal or organizational challenge before you, begin your quest to gather information. What do you know? What do you remember? What can you find out? The word research literally means to re-search. In this first stage, you are looking for things which already exist. This is not the phase where enlightened creative thinking occurs. You may be deliriously exuberant with all that you find, but the real *a-ha* happens a bit later. Step one is information gathering.

Step #2 is a passive process somewhat beyond your control. You have put all of the ingredients (information) into the crock pot. Now it's time to let the stew simmer. It's time to let your unconscious mind do its thing. In that vast warehouse of spongy gray matter, your ideas are associating at will without self-censorship. Be careful not to stifle and snuff out your own tender sparks of creative thought before they ever see the light of day. The conversation with yourself usually goes something like, "Hey, I've got an idea. No, wait. I don't think so. That will never work. It's probably not a good idea." Why do this to yourself? Go ahead! Embrace your preliminary creative thoughts; don't criticize them. Allow the time necessary for the crock pot to cook the stew. Have you ever heard a brilliant presentation that sounds quite similar to ideas and thoughts that you once had but prematurely discarded?

"In the work of every genius,
we recognize our own rejected thoughts."
– Ralph Waldo Emerson

Step #3 is when putting all of the pieces together leads to the A-HA experience! You have gathered the ingredients, you have thrown them into the pot, and you have let them simmer. Then, without warning and from out of the blue, as plain as the back of your hand and as seemingly obvious as the nose on your face, the light bulb brightly shines and you exclaim, "I've got it, I've got an idea!"

In the simplest of explanations, here's what happened. You have connected the seemingly unconnected, bringing previously unrelated things into a new relationship. In our brains, when a nerve impulse fires and connects two previously unconnected neurons, a new junction is established. This new junction is called a synapse. And this joining together, this human hot-wiring, is the blueprint of creativity.

"The human mind, once stretched to a new idea,
never goes back to its original dimension."
– Oliver Wendell Holmes

#7 Creativity Concept: Creative Leadership Moves Forward Despite Frustrations

The Frustration of Creative Thought

When you have reached the limitations of conscious, rational thought and still haven't come up with a new answer or the big idea, it's perfectly natural to become frustrated. Why do most people fail to release their creativity? They give up! They quit not because their problems can't be solved, but because they surrender to anxiety, despair and frustration. Take heart. Frustration is a milestone moment at this stage of the creative thinking process. It means you have exhausted the obvious and now it's time to explore the unknown. This scares the daylights out of most people. (There's that fear we were talking about earlier.) Rather than throwing up your hands in surrender, get excited! The best is yet to come. The answers are there. Be Persistent—Be Patient—Persevere!

The Energy of Creativity

I believe we are surrounded by an abundance of creative energy for which we are engineered to serve as conduits, vehicles and channels. Indeed, to express yourself creatively is the ultimate, divinely-inspired intoxication of the human spirit. This expression may manifest itself in the arts, business, science, sport or in your everyday life. There are those—the leaders—who have willingly allowed themselves to tap into this energy. However, many others tend to fight it, deny it and repel it.

Martha Graham, one of the most influential forces in American Modern Dance, seemed to understand this relationship when she said, "There is a vitality, a life force, an energy, a quickening that is translated through you into action. And because there is only one of you in all time, this expression is unique. If you block it, it will never exist through any other medium and will be lost."

"The best material comes through you, not from you!"
– David Foster

#8 Creativity Concept: The Essence of Creativity Lies in the Waiting

The Freedom to Create

Ideas take time to develop. It could be minutes, hours, days or months before your ideas ripen and reach fruition. But this fickle variable of time flies directly in the face of our society's desire for instant gratification. We need everything yesterday; we're in such a hurry and so busy that we don't allow ourselves the time for idea processing to run its course. Our society has come to recognize and reward the quick decision-makers, therefore we tend to settle for the first right answer we can find.

Creative thinking, in its purest form, implies the need for freedom to explore, to play, to wander and wonder, and to make enlightened discoveries in both your thinking and your doing. Give the people working on the challenge the latitude to experience the power and magnitude of their own creative thinking. It has been said that the act of creating, moving through the process and visibly expressing what lies within us is more important than the creation itself. If you as leader show patience, understand the significance of your frustration and ignore the ever-ticking clock on the wall, you will be rewarded by a more creative staff and organization.

#9 Creativity Concept: See #1 Creative Concept

Write It Down

It's not enough simply to generate an idea. We're all capable of generating ideas—in the car, in the shower or on the golf course. Creativity is action-based! Creative thinking does not take the place of creative doing! Ideas do not take the place of action! You must express the idea in some way. Write it down. Do something with it. Send an e-mail. Tell someone. Make a phone call. Put it in motion.

Write before you forget. It sounds too simple, but I'll bet you have experienced this phenomenon: It's 3:00 a.m. You can't sleep. You're tossing and turning. Suddenly, your mind begins to unravel the mysteries of the universe, figuratively speaking. You're thinking like Einstein, Disney and Socrates all rolled into one. This is big, really big! Then the next morning, you wake up and you can't remember what it was that kept you up all night. It's been said that, "The strongest memory is weaker than the palest ink!" Keep a scratch pad by your bedside. It may sound goofy, but just do it. You'll learn to decipher your midnight scribbles.

Implementation Requires Interaction

Interaction is essential to enhancing the quantitative and qualitative output of your creative thinking. Is it possible to be creative in a vacuum? I suppose so. But is it difficult? Absolutely and without question! Whereas creativity involves thinking, implementation involves doing. Whereas creativity generates and expresses ideas, implementation applies those ideas. Whereas creativity can be experienced by an individual, implementation requires interaction.

#10 Creativity Concept: Creative Leaders Know How to Get to Carnegie Hall

Your ability to think creatively, whether personally or in the context of your organization, demands effort and attention like any other talent or skill. It may seem awkward at first, but you'll learn to trust in the creative thinking process. Practice, practice and practice again. Once you get the hang of it, share what you have learned with those around you, especially in the workplace where creative thinking is so desperately needed in order to move your organization forward.

The Change-to-Creativity Connection

Author and management guru S. Edwards Deming is right. The two basic rules of life are: 1) Change is inevitable, and 2) Everybody resists change. After all, it is so much easier not to change. Change involves effort. Change involves trying something new. Change involves the unknown. Change conjures up your fear and begs you to avoid risk. Sadly, society's sea of negativity, coupled with the "but we've always done it this way" mentality has knocked the luster from our creative pearl, the hidden gem within each of us. And over time, after years of reinforcement, too many of us have clammed up and actually come to believe, "Oh, I'm not really a creative person." Have the confidence and the courage to rediscover your creativity and assert your creative leadership.

The next chapter by my colleague, Marlon Smith, is an example of using creativity to advance your leadership efforts. Given all of the potential formats for sharing one's thoughts on greatness, for instance, Marlon takes an unusual approach that has powerful results. Was it a risk? Not to Marlon. He is the type of individual that goes beyond embracing change to creating it. In fact, he dedicates a majority of his time to encouraging innovative educational strategies in South Africa. As you read his chapter, see if you can appreciate the confidence and courage behind his work.

We now find ourselves immersed in challenging times, characterized by a new sense of urgency. Global events have caused immediate and sweeping changes in even the most mundane aspects of our daily lives. Nothing is sacred. Everything is fair game. It's time to be proactive rather than reactive. It's time to redefine priorities. It's time to move from concept to implementation. It's time to walk the talk. Is your creative spirit engaged?

"Even if you are on the right track,
you will get run over if you just sit there."
– Will Rogers

CHAPTER SUMMARY

❑ Creative leadership is action-oriented.

❑ Confront your fear and embrace the willingness to fail.

❑ Take purposeful risks and step out of your comfort zone.

❑ Frustration is normal. Be patient. Be persistent. Persevere.

❑ Adopt an attitude of always looking for more than one right answer.

On Greatness

The Voice of Marlon Smith

*"A vision without action is just a dream.
Action without a vision is merely a passing of time.
But a vision with action can change the world."*
– Author Unknown

"I should have gotten an 'A' on my paper. This is crazy! All right, all right, Nolram, get yourself together. Put on your game face. It's Professor Brown versus Nolram! And the stakes are high! This is war!"

Knock! Knock!

"Come in!"

I slowly open the door and walk in. And there's Professor Brown sitting behind his mahogany desk with stacks of books and papers. He doesn't even look up from his paperwork. He just motions for me to sit down.

I sit down and start checking out his office. It's typical. All of the plaques, diplomas and certificates are up on the wall. And look at his bookcase… so many books. I wonder if he's read them all or is just "fronting," pretending like he's some serious scholar.

Like he heard my thoughts, Professor Brown looks up, pauses and takes off his glasses.

"Ah yes, Nolram, I see you staring at my bookcase. I believe reading enhances the creative genius within each of us."

I nod, thinking to myself, I didn't come here for a lecture. Class is over.

"So, to what do I owe the honor of this visit during my office hours?"

I take a deep breath. Here we go.

"Well sir, I got a 'B-' on my paper and I think I should have gotten an 'A.' "

I reach into my book bag and pull out my paper. I hand it to Professor Brown. He starts reviewing his comments. I'm watching his face so I'll know how to counter whatever he says because I want my 'A.'

He flips to the next page, reviewing his comments. I really can't read him.

"You could have done better, Nolram."

He hands my paper back to me.

I'm thinking to myself, this sounds like some reverse psychology, some art of war type of strategy. OK, so how should I play it? Hmmm. Let's throw him off. No, no, that's not it. Let's just be straight up.

"OK, Professor, do you want to hear the truth?"

"Yes, I do."

"Yeah, I probably could have done better, but this is still a good paper. I mean let's be real. Is it really worth the extra time? I mean, let's be honest. School is just about the grades so you can graduate and get the high paying job at some Fortune-500 corporation. Most of us college students are just really passing through."

"Is that why you are here getting an education?"

"Yeah, come on, Professor, let's be real. School is just about the paper."

"What paper?"

"The diploma! Professor, the diploma!"

"Really? So let me understand this. You are just here going through the motions so you can graduate, get your diploma and move on to the ultimate goal of working in Corporate America."

"Yeah, it's all about the Benjamins!"

"The Benjamins?"

I start smiling. "Oh sorry, Professor. It's slang. What I'm saying is that I have to get PAID with a PHAT salary."

He starts to chuckle. "More slang, huh?"

I'm trying to hold a serious face. But I can't hold it any longer. I burst out with a hearty laugh.

"Nolram, I really appreciate your honesty."

"Well, Professor, it's the truth. That's why most students are here. To get the diploma and move on."

"How do you feel about that?"

"I don't know. It's just the way it is."

"Interesting! What you've shared is truly profound. A few years ago, I noticed a difference in the students' attitudes toward their education and extracurricular activities."

"Yeah, Professor, it's deep. There is absolutely no school spirit on this campus."

"So why don't you do something about it, Nolram?"

"What? Now come on, Professor, what can I really do? I mean, what can one person really do?"

"Well, Nolram, history illustrates the power of ONE. Look at all the great men and women of our past. They were just like you and me, ordinary people."

He's definitely piqued my curiosity now. "So what makes the great, GREAT?"

Professor Brown smiles. "That's a magnificent question, 'What makes the great, GREAT?' Well, do you see all of those books in my bookcase?"

I look to my right at the bookcase and say, "Yes."

"Nolram, 90% of those books describe the lives of ordinary people who have done extraordinary things. And to me, that's what makes the great, GREAT! It's making the commitment to step up and fulfill one's true potential."

I reflect for a moment. "OK, that sounds good but what exactly does it mean?"

"Let me ask you a question, Nolram. What did you do yesterday that makes you proud?"

I think to myself, interesting question!

I start retracing the events of yesterday. Nothing special. I rolled out of bed around 8:15 a.m., jumped in the shower and raced to Calculus. I met up with James and David for breakfast. I went to the Chemistry lab which was BORING. I ate lunch with Adrian and then went to Philosophy class where I received my 'B-' paper. I came home, relaxed, and then Paul called. He and the guys were going to the gym so I joined them. I ate dinner, went home, showered, and raced to my study session. Afterward, a few of us went to the game room to play some pool and hit the arcade games.

I look at Professor Brown, who is eyeballing me.

"To be honest, Professor, nothing was really special about yesterday. It was just another typical day of classes, studying and hanging out with friends."

"Well, that's the difference between you and what makes the great, GREAT!"

I sit up in my chair to listen more intently.

"Nolram, you are just going through the motions. It's almost as though you're sleepwalking, just doing the same routine over and over. The first key to being GREAT is: To live a life fully conscious and engaged in each moment."

"What? Of course, I'm conscious. I'm living, right?"

"Yes, you obviously have a life. But what type of life is it? Are you really living with excitement? Think about it."

"Professor, you make it sound like I'm supposed to be walking around happy-go-lucky with a big Kool-Aid smile on my face singing, 'Don't worry! Be happy!' That's just not realistic."

"I do appreciate your perspective. But let me explain this concept from another angle. Later this afternoon, if you were to find out that you have only three months to live, what would you do differently?"

"Only three months left? Well, I would DEFINITELY be more in the moment, going after all my goals, soaking up every minute to the last drop. I would . . ."

I pause. The light bulb is going off. I smile.

Key #1: Live a Life Fully Conscious in the Moment

Professor Brown smiles because he knows I got it. I continue sharing my thoughts. "I would live with more passion. There would be a sense of urgency. I would not take things for granted. I would be more fearless, going after my dreams. I would definitely live more in the moment."

"Exactly! That's it, Nolram! You see, most people live their lives as if they have forever to live. When, in actuality, tomorrow is not promised to any of us. What makes the great, GREAT? It's their appreciation of each and every moment. And that means appreciating everyone whom they encounter as well as everything that they experience because time flies by so quickly."

I frown.

"Do you understand?"

"Umm, not 100%."

"OK, let's look at relationships first. Be honest, when you interact with another person, are you fully present, engaged in the conversation, listening intently to him or her?"

"Hmmm, sometimes I guess." I start laughing. "This is wild. To be honest, Professor, most of the time I'm really more concerned about what I have to share. It's like I'm just waiting for the person whom I'm talking to, to just shut up so that I can say what I have to say."

"Yes, that's how most people live their lives, more concerned about what they have to say rather than really taking the time to understand another perspective. And as a result, true communication is not taking place. Nolram, you're involved with a few student organizations, right?"

"Yes, sir, I'm in a fraternity. I was involved with the student programming board but I just got tired of all the student apathy on this campus so I resigned."

"OK, before we discuss student apathy, let's talk about your fraternity. How many brothers are in your fraternity?"

"We're 34 strong!"

"And of these 33 brothers, how many do you consider to be real close friends?"

"I would probably say that I'm real tight with seven frat brothers."

"Why do you think that is?"

"Well, we have a lot in common, I guess."

"How much do you know about your other 26 brothers?"

"To be honest, not much. I mean, we're part of the same fraternity so we're cool but I really don't know them."

"Isn't it interesting how we can spend time around someone and yet not really know that person?"

"Yeah, it's just a surface connection."

"That is true. Now in order to develop meaningful relationships, a true leader implements Key #2." He waits. "Do you want to know what it is?"

With enthusiasm, I reply, "Yes!"

Key #2: Every Day Connect With Another Person

"OK, Key #2 is: Every day, make the time to really connect with at least one person."

"That sounds great, Professor, but how do you do it? I mean, there are only so many hours in the day."

"As a true leader, you have to think outside the box. You must be creative. For instance, you could eat breakfast, lunch or dinner with a different friend. Or you could study with a different friend. And you exercise, right?"

I nod.

"So you could spend quality time together at the gym."

"These are some good ideas. So, Professor, what you're really saying is for me to be proactive in scheduling my time with friends in activities that I'm already doing."

"Yes, that is correct. However, it is not just about becoming closer with your close friends. You could also choose to enhance your relationships with people with whom you are not so close. Remember this: How do you turn a stranger into an acquaintance?

And how do you turn an acquaintance into a friend? And what about a friend into a life-long friend?"

"I don't know. How?"

"It's simple. By spending more time together communicating, with an emphasis on listening. Communication is the key to unity! And to communicate effectively, you must use your two ears and one mouth in that proportion. Does that make sense?"

"Yes, it does."

"OK, great. So remember Key #2: Every day, make the time to really connect with at least one person. Now let's talk about your decision to resign from the student programming board because of the lack of school spirit on our campus."

He pauses for a moment. "So why did you quit?"

"QUIT?! Look, Professor, I gave it 100%. And it just became a waste of time."

"Do you believe great leaders are great because things were easy for them?"

"Of course not. They're great because they overcame tremendous trials and tribulations. That's what makes them great."

"Exactly! You see, Nolram, the common denominator shared by great leaders is that they believe persistence always wins in the end. For you truly to maximize your potential, you must ask yourself two questions when dealing with challenges. Question #1 is: 'What can I learn from this situation?' And Question #2 is: 'What can I do differently to produce my desired outcome?' "

"That's an interesting perspective."

"Yes, it is. By asking yourself these two questions on a consistent basis, your life will take on new meaning. You will now appreciate every experience because you view it as an opportunity for growth. And remember, if you are not growing, then you are…"

I hesitate, then respond, "Dying!"

"That's right, Nolram. Now, hear me correctly. I'm not saying that you should rejoin the student programming board. But just remember, for you to be your best, you will have to appreciate and embrace challenges because they help develop your character."

"That's deep. It's like the old cliché, 'A winner never quits and a quitter never wins.' "

"Thanks for sharing that with me, Nolram. You have just stated Key #3."

"Really?"

Key #3: Never Quit

"Absolutely! Key #3 is: 'Never, never, never quit.' That's what makes the great, GREAT. And to be honest, you already have so much leadership potential."

"Thank you, Professor."

"But you know what, Nolram? Everyone has potential."

"So if everyone has potential, why is it that only a few do great things?"

"Wonderful question. What you're really asking is, 'How does a person turn his or her potential into results?' Do you know the answer?"

I start pondering. "I'm thinking hard but nothing is coming to me."

Key #4: Live By The Principles That You Stand For

"Well, the answer is Key #4. And Key #4 is: 'Determine what you stand for and live by those principles every day.' "

"And how do you do that?"

"Nolram, you must ask yourself, 'What do I stand for and how will I live my life?' And after you answer this question, you must take action. To maximize your true potential, you must totally commit to living by these higher standards NOW."

"Professor Brown, you've been asking a lot of thought-provoking questions."

"Yes, Nolram, I have. And it is because questions are so powerful. Unfortunately, most people are not consciously thinking. Rather, they have become creatures of habit, just following the same routine over and over, day after day. By asking yourself these tough questions, you force yourself to think. And that's the most important gift you can give yourself, the gift of conscious thinking. In fact, a powerful question to get in the habit of asking is, 'Why?' Think about it, 'Why are you here?' 'Why do you do what you do?'"

I smile. "Yeah, I remember the first question that you asked me, 'So Nolram, why are you getting an education?' "

He smiles, too. "Exactly, you remember. Now, in order to maximize your true potential, Nolram, you must commit to 1) asking empowering questions, 2) creating memorable experiences, 3) appreciating your relationships, and 4) not getting caught up in the busy-ness of life."

"Busy-ness of life? What exactly does that mean?"

"Many people never fulfill their true potential because they do not put first things first and make their goals a priority. Nolram, do you keep a journal?"

"No."

"Well, I highly suggest it."

"Why?"

"Think about this. How do you have a successful life? Many successful months. And how do you have a successful month? "

I nod my head.

"That's right, by having successful weeks. And how do you have a successful week?"

I smile and reply, "Many successful days."

"That is correct. So do you now understand why keeping a journal is so important?"

"Yes, so that I can focus on the positive things of each day as well as reflect upon how I moved through various challenges. Now that sounds great and all but how do I journal effectively? I mean, do I just write down everything that's happened during that day?"

"Well, there's not just one right way to journal. For me, I have a process that I follow every day. And it has made a difference in my life. I suggest you find a quiet location and ask yourself a few profound questions."

He opens up his desk drawer and hands a card to me.

On the card, it reads:

Journal Questions:
1. *What makes me feel grateful today?*
2. *What have I learned today?*
3. *What have I enjoyed doing today?*
4. *What is something that makes me proud?*
5. *What have I done today for someone else?*
6. *What have I done today to really make a difference as a leader?*
7. *What are the blessings in my life right now?*
8. *Who have I really connected with today and what did I do to strengthen our relationship?*
9. *What is special about today?*
10. *Today, what is my treat for me?*

I look up from the card.

Professor Brown is smiling. "Every day, I pick at least three questions and write my answers in my journal. I've been doing this for the last twenty-three years and it has transformed my life."

"That's awesome. But what is Question 10 really about? A treat for me? I don't understand."

Key #5: Enjoy A Daily Treat Every Day

"Well, Nolram, to maximize your true potential, you need to remember Key #5: 'I must be good to me and enjoy the journey of life.' Otherwise, if you are not good to yourself, you won't be able to be good to anyone else. So enjoy a daily treat. It could be going for a walk through the park or enjoying a cold slurpee from 7-Eleven or even listening to your favorite CDs for 30 minutes. It can be anything as long as it makes you feel good and is good for you."

"Wow! That really makes sense! I see so many student leaders stressed out all the time because they're so swamped."

"Yes, it's very unfortunate."

I sigh and shake my head.

"Nolram, it appears that you've learned a lot during this conversation."

"Yes, I have."

"Please share some of those highlights with me."

I take a deep breath. "OK, Professor! Basically, I've learned what makes the great, GREAT! It all comes down to the 5 Keys."

"Do you remember them?"

"I think so. Key #1 is: Live a life fully conscious in the moment."

"Excellent!"

"OK, I really like Key #2. Key #2 is: Every day, make the time to really connect with at least one person."

"Why do you like this key so much?"

"Well, it's really going to add spice to my life because I'll strengthen many close relationships and create some new friendships, too."

"And that, Nolram, is true living."

"Yes, it is. OK, two down, three more to go. Give me a minute to remember Key #3. Come on now, let's get busy. Pump it up! Pump it up!"

Professor Brown is smiling. "More slang, Nolram?"

I start laughing. "Yes, Professor!"

"It seems that you are really enjoying these keys, Nolram."

"Yes Professor, these are some incredible insights. I wish I had learned these concepts when I was in junior high school. It would have made a huge difference in my life."

Professor Brown nods.

"OK, I got it. Key #3 is: Never, never, never quit because a winner never quits and a quitter never wins."

"I like that additional phrase."

"I do, too, because it's real. OK, Key #4 is answering the question, 'What do I stand for and how will I live my life?' "

"And after you answer that question, what must you do?"

"I must totally live by these principles every day."

"That's correct. And now, what is Key #5?"

I sit up in my chair and take a deep breath.

"Key #5 is: I must be good to me."

"You did it, Nolram. Congratulations! Now turn the card over."

I turn the card over and read:

KEYS FOR MAKING THE GREAT, GREAT!

Key #1 – I live a life being fully conscious and engaged in each and every moment.

Key #2 – Every day, I make time to really connect with at least one person.

Key #3 – I will never, never, never quit because challenges make me grow.

Key #4 – I determine what I stand for and live by these leadership principles.

Key #5 – I treat myself every day because I deserve to enjoy the journey through life.

"Thank you, Professor Brown."

"Nolram, carry this card with you and look at it at least three times a day. Do it for the next thirty days and it will become a habit. Commit to do this because whatever you do consistently for thirty days becomes a habit. So do it."

"Thank you, I will. In fact, I'm going to write these five keys on poster boards and put them up on my bedroom wall."

"That's an excellent idea."

I stand up, getting ready to leave. As I walk toward the door, Professor Brown says, "Nolram, didn't you come here to get your grade changed?"

I turn around.

He's staring right at me. "You walked into my office pumped up to get your 'A.'"

I smile. "Professor, that sounds like slang."

"What can I say, Nolram? I'm a quick learner."

"Yes, that was my intention. In fact, it was war. That's how bad I wanted my 'A.' But after this conversation, I have been so enlightened that it's not even appropriate to ask to have my grade changed."

"Why not?"

"Because…" I hesitate and then continue, "What makes the great, GREAT?"

Silence fills the room.

I smile and say, "It's all about stepping up and living a life of excellence. No more skating by, trying to get over. That's what makes the great, GREAT!"

Professor Brown quickly stands up and walks around his desk toward me.

He stops right in front of me.

"Yes, you are correct, Nolram. That's what makes the great, GREAT. And Nolram, there is another invaluable lesson that will also enhance your life."

I'm all ears, listening intently.

"Nolram, every situation, every encounter, happens not by luck or chance but by divine intervention. You walked into my office initially to get your grade changed. But now you are leaving with a clear understanding of how to be a great leader."

He pauses.

"Live your life with the understanding that everything happens for a reason. And with this mindset, you will see beyond each and every situation and discover more lessons for your personal growth on this journey called LIFE!"

He extends his hand.

We shake hands.

"Live your life with purpose!"

"I will."

CHAPTER SUMMARY

❑ Unlock your greatness within by moving through fear.

❑ Accept the challenge and be an ordinary person who does extraordinary things.

❑ Live in the moment and your life will take on new meaning.

❑ Each and every experience is an opportunity for growth.

❑ Now is the time to step up and maximize your true potential.

8

On Relationships

The Voice of David D. Coleman

There once was a farmer and a lazy mule named Jack. For years, the farmer tirelessly tried to motivate his prized mule to do a bit of work around the farm. His efforts went for naught, however, as Jack was just too darn lethargic. One day, the farmer had an idea. He decided to enter Jack in the Kentucky Derby.

Six months prior to race day, he began a strict training regimen with Jack. He rose early each morning, strolled to the barn, saddled him and took him on a long walk. Race day finally arrived and the farmer proudly escorted Jack to the starting gate, where he took his place alongside seventeen of the finest thoroughbred racing horses in the world. The starting gates were opened and they were off! As expected, the thoroughbreds bolted into a commanding lead and in an instant were nearing the first turn. Jack, however, was just beginning to mosey out from the starting gate. Mere moments later, the stallions had reached the halfway point as Jack approached the first turn. The pack pounded the turf as they neared the third turn, but alas, Jack labored aimlessly between the first turn and the halfway point, surveying the crowd and enjoying the scenery. In a few seconds, the horses sprinted down the home stretch and blazed across the finish line in a heart-stopping photo finish. Jack gazed across the infield, viewed the finish and heard the roaring crowd. He picked up his pace a bit and fifteen minutes later he finally finished the race. There was the slightest bounce in his step and he held his head just a bit higher.

As expected, the media converged on the farmer in a feeding frenzy, each reporter anxious to be the first to ask him why he had entered his mule in a race he knew the animal had no chance of winning. The farmer's answer was short, simple and poignant: "Because I thought the association would do him some good!"

And it worked! When they returned to the farm, Jack and his owner felt a new sense of pride and kindred spirit. They were a team, and Jack couldn't do enough to help around the farm. His newfound sense of purpose made him feel important and needed.

What associations with others have you had in your life that have done you some good? Think for a moment of all the ways you were changed and how you changed others as a result. Also consider the many role models in your life. What did you learn from your association with them? As you've guessed, association is just another way to describe a connection fostered through intentional and unintentional communication with another person or organization.

Being in "association" with someone or an organization
at a variety of levels is another way
to describe the concept of a relationship.

Relationships Make the Leader

No matter what your career, stage of development or leadership position, one thing will remain constant for the rest of your life: you will have to develop, maintain and excel in interpersonal relationships. Each of us carries with us a bit of every person we have ever met; we should see ourselves as human sponges, ready to take in as much as we can from every single interaction. However, as a leader, you may not always feel like playing! You might not see the value in pursuing relationships with everyone you meet. Although understandable, your success as a difference-maker may very well depend on changing your perspective to one that can recognize the often unrecognizable value of effective interpersonal relationships.

Specifically, the ability to establish and maintain healthy relationships with those you work with, live with, go to class with, and the like, is a reflection of your *desire* to establish and maintain those relationships. How much do you really think your motivation matters? You've heard the saying, "Don't kid a kidder?" Well, consider the impact of a sincerely motivated human being trying to get to know you and one whose motives you question. With the latter, your conversations are more guarded. You hear "noise" every time you interact (i.e. What does he really want from me? or Should I be questioning what I'm being told?) Yet, when you sense a genuine invitation to interact, you are more likely to take your conversations deeper and listen more actively to the real message without looking for hidden messages.

It is a fact of life that you will interact with other people around you. There's no avoiding those that provide services to you, work in or near your office, live where you live, teach your children, marry your cousins, etc. People are social beings who communicate intentionally with the people around them. The quality of these communications—or the extent to which they are maintained—is a choice. In fact, it's your choice. However, as a leader you don't often get to choose the amount of time you spend fostering or maintaining relationships with others, especially when it comes to more structured environments or organizations. You get who you get. You can train them, encourage them and make them feel valued, but you can't ignore their presence. You need to interact. A fundamental understanding of how relationships are established, developed and advanced will benefit your ability to maximize other's potential, as opposed to, merely tolerating it.

Another reason to work toward enhanced interpersonal relationships is to build a solid foundation of trust within your relationships. It is much more productive to disagree and share different viewpoints when a foundation of mutual positive regard has already been established. Knowing that relationships are built in a predictable five stage progression allows you to identify where you are with an individual and what might come next. Leaders often make the mistake of assuming there is a level of trust established between them and their associates, for instance, when what is actually established is their respect for authority. There is a difference. Consider how the following stages of relationship development can help you to advance your relationships. The five stages of relationships are predictable and an inevitable part of significant human interactions.

THE FIVE STAGES OF A RELATIONSHIP

Think of someone you know and your history with that individual. Can you think of examples that correspond to the following stages of a relationship? Note that the duration of each stage depends upon the persons involved and the situation at hand. You will find that every relationship in which you are involved—whether personal, professional or volunteer—involves these five stages.

Initial Interest – Stage One

In the initial stage of a relationship, your *interest* is sparked immediately, leading you to feel an instant and commanding attraction. (In a romantic relationship, this stage would be referred to as "infatuation.") Your interest in the activity, organization or group which has caught your attention is all consuming, leading you to think constantly about becoming more seriously involved—maybe even serving as the leader. You visualize how and where you might be able to lead and how you might grow as a person in the process.

Discovery – Stage Two

In the process of *discovering* more about the organization, you actually join and learn your way around. During this stage, you begin to learn more about the position you have accepted and those whom you have been chosen to lead, manage, supervise or follow. Strengths and weaknesses, opportunities and limitations become clearer and more apparent as you begin to focus on and comprehend the overall picture. You accept that human beings have faults and that you need to collect more information in order to make sound decisions for yourself and others.

Reality – Stage Three

In the third stage of a relationship, you have come to understand the *reality* of the situation in which you find yourself. You have gathered all of the information you need in order to see clearly the opportunity before you. You have been exposed to those involved in the organization long enough to understand fully their (and your own) strengths, weaknesses, potential, opportunities and limitations. You are now thinking clearly, no longer blinded by the emotion that accompanied your initial interest. You ask those you lead questions such as "Am I meeting your expectations?" "What expectations did you have?" "Have your expectations and assumptions changed as a result of your experience so far?"

Decision – Stage Four

You come next to a critical point in your involvement, the point at which you must *decide* either to become a true leader of the organization or terminate your involvement (or someone else's!) Here you must ask yourself a few important questions: "Why do I want to lead?" "What have I learned about myself?" "Am I prepared to see this through to its successful, logical conclusion even if the going gets tough?" People often avoid this stage for as long as possible due to the emotional and personal ramifications. Inevitably, the consequence of the decisions you make will cause elation or disappointment, either for yourself or others; you may also challenge everyone involved to a new level of productivity. Some thrive under such pressure, though others fear the unknown and find leading others through it to be an intimidating burden.

Commitment – Stage Five

Finally, you make a decision to *commit* yourself. Whether for personal or business reasons, you enter into a partnership with others and a contract with yourself. Once a commitment has been made, one of three outcomes is likely. First, the relationship will grow, continuously improving for you and for others. Second, the relationship will hit a "maintenance" plateau, which is like treading water. You aren't swimming, you aren't sinking, you're just hanging there. Third, the relationship will regress and rapidly deteriorate. This outcome manifests itself in the form of painful conflicts, a loss of support, a drop in membership or a failed business venture, none of which are particularly enticing options. You want to commit to establishing relationships that will grow knowing that this may take the most amount of effort when compared to the other options.

You will only truly comprehend the
depth of your character when you face adversity.

Awareness of the above five stages and what to expect from each puts you in a better position to maintain, and yes, control the direction of your interactions. Armed with knowledge, you will have the poise and the foresight necessary to make sound decisions. You have the responsibility to enter into relationships with open eyes.

Why Leaders Take the Blame

By definition, a leader attempts to influence people and move them to realize a shared vision. If those you lead fail to achieve the desired outcome, the blame will fall upon you simply because of the position you hold—that of leader. You've probably already discovered this reality. Not everyone wants to assume the manager, coordinator, chairperson or director roles, for instance, for this very reason. They don't want to take the hit when the system breaks down. However, it is this very responsibility which elevates you to the leadership position and serves as a powerful motivating force. You recognize that there is a price to pay for the choice of leadership.

Being a leader also means you are held to a higher standard and to a greater degree of accountability with regard to your interpersonal relationships. People are watching from every direction. How do you lead a team? How do you handle conflict among your organization members? What do you do to inspire others to improve their interpersonal relationships in the face of adversity?

It is easy to lead and maintain effective relationships when everything is progressing as planned. It is a far greater challenge to make a positive impact and effective decisions during a time of distress or crisis. Unfortunately, not all leaders know how to identify when their organization is in a state of relationship distress or crisis. It's not as easy as reading the bottom line or reading a spreadsheet. To know when your relationships are in need of repair, you need to know what healthy ones look like.

Healthy Leadership Relationships

All healthy relationships, whether personal, social or business, share five common characteristics: *trust, respect, intimacy, passion* and *commitment*. The quickest way to ascertain and maintain the health of a relationship is to remember this simple check and balance system. In a healthy relationship, the stronger person (the one with the healthier balance of mind, body and spirit) takes care of the weaker person. In an unhealthy relationship, the stronger person takes advantage of the weaker one. By "strong," I don't mean brute physical strength, or an ability to dominate. Rather, I mean the strength that is defined by character, integrity, honesty and compassion, as well as the capacity to think and act in a manner that takes the interests and well being of others into consideration.

*Trust is the confidence to believe that a person's words
and actions will be what they say they will be.*

Once we lose trust in a person or a situation, it frequently takes a great deal of time, patience and consistent, error-free behavior before we begin to trust again. Trust is the core of every relationship, the glue that holds it together. It motivates people to perform at higher levels without regard to who will get the credit; those who work for leaders they trust feel as though their efforts are appreciated and their ideas valued.

Respect is mutual, equal and earned. Each day that you remain in association with someone who does not respect you, you are in danger of two possible consequences. First, you will lose valuable self-esteem, which is extremely difficult to restore. Second, you may try to convince yourself that you should settle for the way things are, on the assumption that no one gets all the respect they deserve. "Sure, I could be treated better or treat others better," you might think. "But I have it pretty good, and so do they. We should be thankful for that." My many years as a relationship expert forces me to challenge you to raise the bar! Work to earn the respect of others and treat others only with respect, regardless of how they treat you.

> *"The way you see people is how you treat people.*
> *How you treat people is what they become."*
> *– Goethe*

Another characteristic of a healthy relationship is *intimacy*—not necessarily "romantic interest!" Rather, intimacy as used here involves the non-physical aspects of a relationship, aspects that include honest and direct communication, eye contact, the incorporation of appropriate humor and a true and shared sense of faith. It is the desire to grow closer, stronger, more comfortable and more committed as individuals working together for the same cause.

The fourth characteristic to achieve in your interpersonal relationships is that of *passion*. This emotion is a significant characteristic to healthy relationships and the primary force behind our drive to lead. It incorporates spiritual, intellectual, emotional and physical preparation and commitment to lead others toward the pursuit of excellence and success by using the proper methods at the appropriate times. It means being able to balance ambition with compassion, success with failure, and challenge with support.

When you consider all four characteristics mentioned thus far (trust, respect, intimacy and passion) you get the feeling that collectively they lead to something larger than their separate values. The characteristic of *commitment* is the period at the end of the sentence. It is the culminating statement, the evidence that you are involved in this endeavor for the long haul. Commitment is insepa-rable from trust and supersedes all other characteristics. It is a personal guarantee that you will be there for better or worse until the outcome is realized or a new direction is agreed upon.

Commitment often requires you to reprioritize your life in order to emphasize your responsibilities and the contract you have entered into with yourself and with others.

Is it no wonder this characteristic also represents the final stage of the five stages of relationship building as mentioned above?

How to Enhance Your Relationships

Assuming you as the leader are invested in having healthy relationships, the question of *How?* comes into play. You have been a communicator all of your life. Sometimes you have done it brilliantly and at other times, you may have made a mistake or two. There is no one way to improve your relationships. There is no timeline either. There are behaviors and attitudes, however, that will increase your odds of better quality relationships—six of which are suggested below.

SIX CLIFF NOTES ON RELATIONSHIP BUILDING

Trying to remember all of this is like trying to remember the intricacies of a golf swing, if you think about everything you need to do to form a correct swing and hit the ball flush, you will be overcome by paralysis. If, however, you trust your training, experience and instincts and just swing freely, you will experience rewarding results.

Tip #1: When Someone Shows You Their True Self, Believe Them

A person can only maintain a facade for so long before their true character reveals itself. This will usually occur during a time of great stress or conflict. When that happens, you will know exactly with whom you are dealing.

Tip #2: Focus on What You Have Control Over

You cannot control another person's words, actions or feelings, nor are you responsible for them. You can only work to manage your own behavior and lead with integrity.

Tip #3: A Person of Integrity Doesn't Deal in Character Debates

During a conflict, never attack another person's character. Keep to the point at hand and don't deviate. You can apologize for something said in anger, but you can never take it back. It leaves a lasting imprint. Be specific about behaviors you are trying to challenge, but avoid general statements (i.e. You are lazy.) that are intended to belittle the other person. Leaders build character, they don't destroy the basic human rights of those around them.

Tip #4: Don't Blame Others Until You've Looked in the Mirror First

When you point fingers and place the blame on others, you may be disappointed to discover the same weaknesses within yourself. So before you approach someone else about an error in their judgment, thought or action, take a good hard look at your own work. It is often thought the very weaknesses we see in others are those we subconsciously question in ourselves. Positive talk is always more productive and opens the door for deeper relationships.

Tip #5: Life Isn't a Game of Chance

Leadership isn't a game. You are trying to achieve measurable results. There are tough decisions to make and not everyone is going to have their own agendas brought forward. This is the point. Prepare yourself not to be popular. Someone else doesn't get to step in and be "It" if they don't like the way you're leading. Leadership isn't a popularity contest. You have taken an oath to do the best possible job you can—that's why you're reading this book. You have put yourself in a position to make tough decisions; others have put their faith in you. Not everyone will like what you do. Be prepared to defend your actions and decisions based upon sound moral principles. Remember this: if you are not the lead dog on the sled team, the view will never change!

Tip #6: Control Arises from Fear

The desire to control stems from fear; fear develops from lack of faith. People fear two basic things: losing something they already have and not getting something they truly want. When someone tries to control you, try to discover which he or she fears the most and the answer to the dilemma should manifest itself with ease. For example, ask yourself when having difficulties in a relationship with someone, "What are they afraid of?" It's a strange thought because you're normal reaction is to be defensive. Move beyond defensiveness. Reason out your discrepancies until you can see the bottom line or emotional foundation. This is also called insight.

Developing as a Leader

Successful leaders are those that truly have insight into the human personality. They are able to walk in other's shoes and to leave interactions with everyone's basic human needs in tack. They don't destroy nor manipulate those around them. Leaders don't ignore how relationships and individuals change—in fact, they encourage it. Advancing within an organization where you assume more and more responsibility, for instance, will alter how others view you and impact your communication patterns with them. I have articulated below the five stage pattern that typically accompanies this kind of progression or leadership development. Again, as you review this model, consider where you are in relationship to those you lead.

STAGES OF LEADERSHIP DEVELOPMENT

As you review these stages below, consider how they relate to the other contextual frameworks we have already discussed. You can clearly draw parallels to the stages of relationship building which clearly suggests the intentional role you can play in moving relationships to higher levels. The five stages a leader will experience include:

1. Fear and Apprehension
2. Acclimation
3. Experimentation
4. Solidification
5. Renewed Vision or Closure

Stage 1: Fear and Apprehension

We are often struck by fear and apprehension when we accept and commit to a position of leadership or engage in a new relationship. Your unconscious voice begins to ask, *Can I do this? Am I really the one to lead this group? What is my motivation? Why am I the leader and not simply a team member? Will they respect me?* or *Will I respect them?* Uncertainty and concern for how you are perceived begins most leadership positions.

Stage 2: Acclimation

Acclimation occurs as you become more comfortable with your new role. You form basic relationships and begin to recognize the strengths and weaknesses of everyone involved, including yourself. You acquire a sense of the organization's history and begin forming a rudimentary plan and strategy for implementing change. During this stage, you begin to feel a sense of belonging and purpose. You begin to believe you can be successful in your new endeavor.

Stage 3: Experimentation

As you become secure in your new situation and relationships, you feel comfortable with experimentation, or taking risks which define who you are as a person and as a leader. You will lead by example, remaining humble when successful and taking responsibility when not. For those who embrace challenge and change, this is an exciting time. For those who crave the security that comes with accepting the status quo, it can be a long and arduous process. During this phase, either by trial and error or by modeling others, you begin to develop your own personal leadership style and relationship patterns. Your style may end up being your own creation or an eclectic hybrid of your experiences.

Stage 4: Solidification

In this stage, you mature and come into your own as a person, partner and leader. You have subscribed to a style of leadership and communication that makes you feel confident. You have become proficient at what you do and are considered a true leader in your chosen area of expertise. Others may flock to work for or with you as they know they will be treated with respect, their ideas fully considered and they will be made to feel as though they have a worthwhile contribution to make. They know they matter because you make them feel that way. You take calculated risks and employ honesty and integrity to bring about positive change without endangering your relationships, situation or membership.

Stage 5: Closure or Refined Vision

Ultimately, in any leadership position, you will reach the stage when you begin to believe that closure or refined vision is necessary. It is either time to move on (for your own good and that of the organization) or to redefine your goals and role as you hit an impasse. You can no longer be challenged personally in your current situation or lead others to a new level of excellence. Your challenge has been met and your resources have been thoroughly tapped.

Back on Track

No one said being a leader was going to be easy. As is being discussed throughout this book, it takes a host of understandings, attitudes and skills. This chapter has dealt with the significance of surrounding yourself with healthy productive relationships—or, associations. I have attempted to demonstrate that many interpersonal relationships, both personal and professional, occur in a predictable stage, as does the development of your leadership. Being aware of these concepts allows you to not only stay in the race, but to know where the start and finish line are located.

The question remains, *Are you in the race to win, place or show?* Remember the farmer and his mule named Jack? Despite the fact that the farmer knew his mule was way out of his league, he entered him in the Kentucky Derby. He trained Jack. He took care of Jack. He led Jack to the starting gate. He also knew Jack was there for a greater good. It wasn't about beating the finest thoroughbred race horses in the world, it was about believing they all had something that Jack needed—a goal and the belief that each one of them would beat out their competition. The farmer put his mule in a position to associate with winners. Do you want to be remembered as an exceptional leader who truly made a difference or one who watched from the stands?

> *"It truly takes more nobility of character to confront and resolve [relationship issues] than it does to continue to diligently work for the many projects and people out there."*
>
> – Stephen R. Covey
> in The 7 Habits of Highly Effective People

CHAPTER SUMMARY

❑ Your associations will influence your potential to make a difference.

❑ There are five stages to building significant relationships.

❑ In times of adversity, your relationship skills can best be challenged and developed.

❑ By employing the six cliff notes on relationship building you can become a better leader.

❑ Leadership does not happen in isolation. You need people to lead.

. . . .

9

On Becoming an Ethical Leader
The Voice of Will S. Keim, Ph.D.

"We give every appearance of sleepwalking through a dangerous passage of history. We see life-threatening problems, but we do not react. We are anxious, but immobilized.

I do not find the problems themselves as frightening as the questions they raise concerning our capacity to gather our forces and act...Suppose that we have lost the capacity to motivate ourselves for arduous exertions on behalf of the group?"

In 1990, Dr. John W. Gardner, noted author, psychologist, veteran, and former Secretary of Health, Education, and Welfare wrote the above prophetic and cautionary introduction to the book, *On Leadership*. Clearly these are questions we would ask even under normal circumstances. But after the horrific acts of September 11, 2001, we must all stand before the mirror of self-examination, search our deepest souls and ask:

- Can I motivate myself to act on behalf of the larger good?
- What am I willing to sacrifice myself for?
- What can I do?
- Does one person really make a difference?
- How does one person become an ethical leader in today's complex world?

During our time together in this chapter, I will provide support for the following answers to the questions above:

- Yes...the time is now...this is the moment!
- Your deepest-held beliefs, values, and principles!
- Anything you commit yourself to do!
- A world of difference!
- Let me show you...

This chapter is devoted to helping you learn to actualize your full potential for leadership; it concerns the development of your character, and it teaches you a four-step ethical model for decision-making that leaders can use in any situation to resolve intra-personal, interpersonal and group conflict situations in a community-building and enhancing manner.

There are some basic assumptions I would like you to consider before we move on. These are:

- **Leadership without ethics is despotism.**
- **Ethical leadership without character is like a home built on sand; it will not stand the test of time.**
- **Leadership, ethics and character without community exist only in the person and are therefore isolated concepts rather than lived realities.**

As an educator, I want to teach you to become an ethical leader who participates in the creation of genuine human community, where individuals can become women and men of character. This is my purpose in this chapter and in my life as an educator. I am not talking about a quick fix. Rather, I offer you tools that you may use first to become a contributor to the common good and then to emerge as a leader who inspires others to make a difference. When will this process be completed? When you take your last breath! I am proposing a lifetime of learning, a journey toward a world lived in community with others. If this seems idealistic or unattainable, consider the alternative to genuine human community: isolation, fear and hopelessness. Can one live like that? Consider the words of Laura Pappano in her book, *The Connection Gap*:

> *We end up belonging to and identifying with a mass market, a faceless public. We bond in our minds through orchestrated public experiences that we consume privately. We feel familiar, even intimate, with people who arrive every evening on our television screens, who speak with us every morning via radio as we shower or commute, who are faithfully online, who come alive on the big screen and whom we fret over and identify with through the pages of celebrity magazines. We love Oprah (some even expect her to handle our bills.) Prepubescent girls are crazy for Leo. We rely on Don Imus to grouse and Dr. Laura to set us straight. These— and many others—are important voices in national life. But even as we identify with particular public figures, we remain alone. We may write, call in, appear in the studio audience, but it remains a one-way relationship that cannot replace local ties. And yet it seems easier to engage as part of this super-public than as part of a real community...*

Leaders must engage in the community; ethical leaders engage ethically and responsibly. But how? When? With whom? We will tackle these questions together on the path to becoming ethical leaders. But first we must ask Why?

- *Why be concerned with the character issue?*
- *Why engage ethically with others in genuine community?*
- *Why connect at all when it is easier not to?*

> **"Ethics** *is the discipline dealing with what is good and bad and with moral duty and obligation."*
> *– (Webster's, p. 392)*

Ethics concerns a set of moral principles or values. Ethics are principles of conduct governing individuals or groups. As leaders of industry, emerging student leaders, organizational leaders and leaders of our own lives, we must ask the fundamental question, Why engage ethically? It is my belief that the answer is straight forward. To not do so results in anarchy, with and between persons. Chaos is a wonderful theory, but rarely results in a meaningful course of ethical action. We engage in ethical connections with others not only because it gives us personal fulfillment but also because it gives our lives meaning, purpose and direction toward a common good.

> *"All real life is encounter. The fundamental fact of human existence is person with person."*
>
> – *Martin Buber*

Real life—yours and mine—involves relationships with others. Born out of the relationship between one person and another, we naturally seek relationships with other human beings. We seek intimacy and relation our entire lives. Relationships are as important to human beings as air, water and food: not options but necessities. So it is with relationships and connections with others. Real life is best lived out in quality interpersonal relationships within a larger community of connections between persons and groups.

Finally, why engage with others by connecting in communities driven by character? Heraclitus said, "Character is our destiny." The Rev. Martin Luther King, Jr. said, "Intelligence plus character— that is the goal of a true education." Martin Buber stated, "Education worthy of the name is essentially the education of character." Get it? Rooted in the Greek language, character has come to mean the "constellation of strengths and weaknesses that form and reveal who we are." (Templeton Foundation, Colleges that Develop Character, p.vii). Some say character is what we do when no one is looking. So I ask, **"What shall we do?"**

> *"We are what we repeatedly do."*
>
> – *Aristotle*

I propose that you decide to be an ethical person: a person of good character, a principled, engaged, community-minded person who decides this very day to make a difference not only on your own behalf but for the common good. I want you to see this decision as central to your life today, tomorrow and always. These values are at the very core of your being and are the cornerstone of civilization. With them, we live together in hope. Without them, we tremble alone in fear. It truly is a matter of life and death, this choice between being alone and being engaged, connected or disconnected. No choice is more essential to our survival than this one! So, which will you lead by? Life or death? Consider that the choice of life means to engage in ethical behavior based on principles of character directed toward the common good. Conversely, the choice of death means to refuse to accept personal responsibility for the betterment of the world. Choose life, connection, character, principle, community!

> *"In matters of opinion, swim with the fish;*
> *but in matters of principles,*
> *stand firm like a rock."*
> – Mark Twain

From the Philosophical to the Practical

Learning to lead with ethics and character means learning to make ethical decisions based on a model that facilitates behavior contributing to the common good. I would now like to share with you a Four-Step Model for Ethical Decision-Making that will help you do just that. It is time to move from the philosophical to the practical, from goal to objective. Assuming I have convinced you "Why" we need to become ethical leaders, let us now consider "How," "When," and "With Whom."

> *"No legacy is so rich as honesty."*
> – Shakespeare

The Four Questions of Ethical Decision-Making

The truth is this: ethical leaders must ask themselves four central questions before engaging in actions which will have an impact upon others. I am indebted to Dr. J. Wesley Robb of the University of Southern California for his understanding of the importance of a model for ethical decison-making. Why do we engage in ethical leadership? Because it is the foundation of a civilized society and world. How do we begin this process? By discovering a model for ethical decision-making and putting it into practice. When do we do this? Now and forevermore. And with whom? With every person who is willing to engage with us in the creation of communities based on character for enhancement of the common good.

> *"The journey of a thousand miles*
> *begins beneath your feet."*
> *– Lao Tzu in the Tao Te Ching*

For the emerging leader, this process might seem daunting. The process may also seem daunting if you have been the leader of an organization for many years. There are challenges and obstacles on the way of turning a vision into a reality and of leading with integrity, morality and a steady sense of right and wrong. Whether you have had a successful history or not, the important thing is to get started. You might be wondering:

- *How do I follow my voice, my plan, and not the one my parents or guardians laid out for me?*

- *How can I make my mark on the world?*

- *Is there more to life than making money?*

- *How do I make an ethical decision in today's fast-paced world?*

It would be fabulous if I could give you a ready-wrapped answer-to-go to these and many other questions you will ask yourself late in the night. It has been my experience that simple solutions do not fit complex problems. I can, however, share with you a framework that will give your decision-making a system, a plan, that will help you develop as an ethical leader. I've also provided a variety of examples to illustrate how to use the following four questions on your way to making an ethical decision:

The Essential Questions of Ethical Leadership:

1. *What is my motive in doing this act? What is my intention?*
2. *What is the applicable law or policy governing this act?*
3. *What are the possible consequences of my actions?*
4. *What are my moral principles regarding this act?*

We can, and must, make a positive impact on the world by making ethical decisions which establish an integrity, a "life-giving" dimension to our interactions with others. You can live well and prosper by doing what is right, looking out for your neighbor's well-being as well as your own. Below are three examples which demonstrate how to apply the above essential questions to life situations.

Potential Action: Cheat on a test.

- *What is my motive?* To do better on the test and make up for a lack of honest preparation.
- *What is applicable law or policy?* The Honor Code forbids cheating and may demand my suspension if my cheating comes to light.
- *What are the possible consequences?* A better grade or suspension and embarrassment.
- *What are my moral principles regarding cheating?* I am tempted, but I was taught cheating was wrong.

Problem areas include: What if I don't care about being caught? What if I was not taught that cheating is wrong? But these questions prove my point: You can only ignore the fact that cheating is wrong if you are unethical, unprincipled and a person of questionable character. Students sometimes tell me, "There are usually a number of choices that could be ethical and right given a slight interpretation of the circumstances." I respond, "You are right...but there is always one choice a little more right than the others."

Another Potential Action: Drop GHB Into Someone's Drink.

- *What is my motive?* Is it intimacy I want? Sex? A relationship? Couldn't these all be better achieved with a conscious and willingly participating partner?

- *What is applicable law or policy?* Drugs are against the law.

- *What are the possible consequences?* I might have sex but I might also be convicted of rape, contributory negligence or wrongful death; these drugs can cause permanent brain damage or even death after even a single use.

- *What are my moral principles?* It seems like a long time ago, but I was taught to treat other people as I would like to be treated.

Potential problem areas include: What if I wasn't taught basic values, such as treating others as I want to be treated? Or what if I was abused and do intend to treat others as I was treated? Again, a lack of character-driven education and unethical choices result in harm for at least one of the parties, proving the point that ethical leadership is needed to teach and make good decisions that do not harm individuals but rather help people to live in community with each other.

Final Potential Action: Feed A Homeless Person.

- *What is my intention?* To help someone out or to put something good on my resume.

- *What is the applicable law or policy?* This is not relevant here.

- *What are the consequences?* He eats and I feel better about myself.

- *What are my moral principles?* I think it is important to take care of those less fortunate than myself.

Potential problem areas include: What if I think people get what they deserve and since this guy is homeless he deserves to go hungry?

What if I don't really care? What if I only want to put something like "Worked with the homeless" on my resume? There is so much that needs to be done that we cannot afford the luxury of worrying about the motivation behind the good action. If the chooser selects isolation and disconnection, someone gets hurt, once again demonstrating the need for ethical conduct for the common good.

"The right thing for the wrong reason is still the right thing."
– Dr. Craig Franz

The Consistency Factor

The above four-question model works. Becoming a person of character and integrity means narrowing the gap between what you say and what you do and increasing your concern for the well-being of others as well as yourself. And now is the time to make that decision to be an ethical leader. Why? Kay Lyons said, "Yesterday is a canceled check; tomorrow is a promissory note; today is the only cash you have—so spend it wisely."

Undoubtedly, the events of September 11, 2001 taught us all how precious life is, how much we should immerse ourselves in the present with our friends and family, and what happens when others choose to act in an immoral, unethical manner. Leadership in the 21st Century demands engagement, integrity and character-driven ethical action. Are you ready? Can you become this kind of leader? The answer, I believe, is a resounding, "Yes!!!" Regardless of your age, position, place of residence (or if you even have one), leadership role, race, religion and the like, I am filled with hope about your potential to enhance your ethical leadership. Becoming a leader with integrity depends upon this understanding:

The Facts of Life

- Say what you mean,
- Do what you say, and
- When you don't, admit it.

No one will ask you to be a saint in order to be a leader. But everyone wants a leader who behaves ethically, who is a man or woman of integrity, whose spirit is governed by character and a deep sense of commitment to community and the common good. And ethical leadership begins with you, right now, right here. Take the first step and begin your journey toward becoming an ethical leader. Do not be immobilized by fear or by the scope of our problems. Do not sleepwalk through history or through your own life. Make your mark by making the decision to care, to hope and to love ... today.

"Success is the peace of mind that comes from knowing
you did the best you were capable of doing and
you are the only person who will ever know that."

– John Wooden

CHAPTER SUMMARY

❑ The discipline of ethics is concerned with making judgments of good and bad, and right and wrong—as well as—moral duty and obligation.

❑ Ethical leaders are not born, rather they are made by a series of decisions and the consequences of those decisions.

❑ Before acting, ask yourself these questions: Why am I doing this? What is the applicable law or policy? What are the potential consequences of my actions? What are my moral principles relevant to my options?

❑ Real life demands authentic relationships with other people lived out in genuine community.

❑ Becoming a person of character and integrity means narrowing the gap between what you say and what you do. It means increasing the amount you care for the well-being of others, as well as yourself.

10

On Leading with Courage

The Voice of Randy Haveson

Courage is not the absence of fear.
Courage is action in the face of fear.

What image pops into your head when you hear the word "courage?" Do you picture the young man in China standing defiantly in front of the tank as it crossed Tianaman Square? Do you remember New York City firefighters rushing into the twin towers of the World Trade Center on September 11, 2001? Do you see a student getting up in front of the class to recite a poem? Or do you think of the Cowardly Lion from the "Wizard of Oz?"

My favorite story of courage is the story of King Arthur, one of the best examples of leadership and courage in literature. As a boy, he loses his brother's sword. Looking for a new one, he comes upon a strange sword sticking out of a stone, puts his hand on its hilt, and pulls it free. He brings the sword to his brother, who realizes what he is holding and says, "Go put it back! Don't you know what this is? This is Excalibur." Arthur, dumbfounded, rushes to return the sword. But Merlin, the great wizard, has seen him; he calls everyone to witness the great event. Pointing to Arthur, he tells the gathered assembly that the boy has taken the sword from the stone.

The people laugh, certain that Arthur is not worthy to perform such a great feat. The other knights try one by one to free the sword from the stone themselves but it doesn't budge. Then Merlin turns to Arthur and says, "Show them."

And here we have Arthur's shining moment of courage: shaking with fear, with all eyes upon him, the young boy puts his hand around the hilt of the sword and easily pulls Excalibur from the stone.

How many of us have faced our own shining moment, aware that we can accomplish the goal, success well within our grasp, only to freeze with fear and walk away? Have you? Courage is the ability to reach for the sword and pull it free, even when to do so is difficult, demanding, frightening. Even a small boy, little more than a squire, has the power to create Camelot. My great hope for you is that you find the courage deep inside yourself to create a Camelot in your own life.

There are many ingredients that go into the makeup of a successful leader: integrity, respect, honor and commitment, among others. Chief among them I believe is courage, an attribute that has been exhibited by every great leader in history. In this chapter, I will show you how to define courage as it applies to you and guide you in incorporating the concept or value of courage into your own life and leadership.

Courage is a trait I have had all of my life, though it wasn't until I was confronted with a life-threatening event that I truly understood its power. As an adolescent, I made poor decisions, a pattern of self-sabotage that culminated in May of 1984 with expulsion (my second) from a major university, getting fired from my pizza delivery job, and the overwhelming feeling that life just wasn't worth living anymore. I remember sitting on the edge of my bed with the expulsion letter from San Diego State and a knife. I knew enough about suicide to know how to get the job done on the first try. I had sat there for a long time when I happened to look up and catch my reflection in the bathroom mirror.

"Oh, my God," I said to myself. "What happened to you?"

I didn't recognize the person looking back at me in the mirror. I flashed back to my childhood. Where was that cute little kid with the brown corduroy pants, the little white polo shirt, and the *Hush Puppy* shoes? Where was that easy laugh, the broad smile, and the sparkling eyes. Suddenly, there in the mirror was this 24-year-old man with long black stringy hair, sunken cheeks, pale skin, with deep black circles under his eyes.

Looking at that gaunt, hopeless man it hit me like a ton of bricks. I had a drug problem! Everything stemmed from that truth. And that's when my desperation and hopelessness turned into fear. I had no idea what to do.

At that critical point, I did the most courageous thing I've ever done in my entire life, before or since: I reached out for help by calling a hotline. The phone had never seemed heavier than it did that night. My heart was racing and my hands shook as it rang. A voice answered, "Be Sober Hotline, can I help you?" "Um…I think I have a drug problem," I said hesitantly, and the hotline volunteer took over from there. She told me about her own experience, she told me where I could go for help, she told me she understood exactly how I was feeling. She gave me the one thing I needed most at that time—hope.

Here I sit, 17 years later, a college graduate with a master's degree in counseling. I have worked as a therapist in a number of different settings. I have been a university administrator (ironic for someone who used to get thrown out of colleges), and today I am the president of my own company. Every step of the way I battled self-doubt, negative thinking and fear. But I've learned to walk through the fear without letting it consume me. I've also learned that as time goes on and my self-confidence grows, it becomes easier to face fear. So yes, I know about courage. And that's why I want to explain how and why I believe this trait is vital on your journey to become a great leader.

No one can expect to lead a life that is free of all stress, smooth sailing all the time, or devoid of difficult decisions. That's not realistic. What is real is your ability to meet these stressful life events armed with the tools you need to be successful. And one of those tools is courage.

Imagine courage is an iceberg. Only its tip is visible above the water line. In the course of a stressful event, we can dive deep into ourselves and discover how much courage we actually possess, hiding just beneath the surface whether we already know that or not. Unfortunately, many of us overlook our strengths, including our courage. Strangely, we never fail to remember each and every one of our shortcomings. So, although some people tend to think it is arrogant to acknowledge our good qualities, I believe that a strong leader—a courageous leader—is confident and aware of their strengths, ready to admit them without self-consciousness.

Learning the Path of Courage and Change

Anytime we make changes in our lives, we leave our "comfort zone" and enter new territory. Yes, that can be terrifying. But if we wait until the fear is gone, we will never move forward. When I speak to friends and colleagues who are unhappy with their jobs, they say, "I know I'm not happy, but at least I have a job." They make excuses for staying put, but in reality their fear has paralyzed them; they cannot move forward. What's missing is their ability to tap into their own courage. Making changes, whether it's in careers, relationships, or unhealthy behaviors is like a snake in the process of shedding its old skin. The old skin is comfortable and has worn well. The new skin is very fragile and sensitive. It might seem safer to keep the old, but in truth the new skin is stronger, requiring only time to develop properly. We must trust in the process of change, having the courage to shed the old and use the strength of the new to free ourselves from that which is holding us back.

THE FIVE KEYS TO COURAGE

Tapping into your courage to make it part of your leadership isn't easy, but it is simple. Here are five ways you can learn to tap into your courage and use it to your advantage in all aspects of your life.

Courage Key #1. Trust

Trust yourself! How many times have you been in a situation, hesitated, then later regretted waiting? We're very good at beating ourselves up for not taking advantage of life's opportunities. I once came across an announcement for a position at a very prestigious university. My first thought was, "Wouldn't it be great to work there?" But then my self-doubt kicked in and I thought, "Yeah, right. Why would they choose me? I used to get kicked out of universities. They would never hire me." So I passed up the chance to apply for the position. At a conference a few months later, I ran into the woman who was in charge of filling the position. I talked to her for a few minutes and she asked why I hadn't applied. I made a few excuses. Then she said, "Actually, I like what I'm hearing from you. The deadline has already passed, but I'd be willing to take your application." So there I was with another decision to make. I applied for the job and I did get an interview, one of three finalists out of 250 applicants. At that point I realized I had already won, whether I got the job or not. And not because of their decision about who might get the job. But because of mine, my decision to step up to the plate.

The Enemy in Your Head

I learned that my own worst enemy lives right between my ears; if I just get out of my own way, I can accomplish anything! No, I didn't get the job. They gave it to one of the other two finalists. Yet my courage had nonetheless been rewarded, not only by the positive response to my application but also by my own sense of accomplishment. Today I trust myself... most of the time.

In 1998, I had a good job at a university where I knew I was making a difference. At the same time, my speaking career was really beginning to take off. I had to make a decision. Should I keep my job at the university, with a full-time paycheck and benefits, or quit to start my own speaking business? I knew I could touch many more lives as a speaker than I could working on a single campus. So I quit my job, moved to Atlanta, and started my own business. I was scared and thought many times that I had made a huge mistake. But I hung in there with my first instinct. I trusted that little voice inside that said, "Go for it!" Years later I find myself with a booming career and now collaborating on a book about leadership with some of the most established, well-respected speakers in the business. And just seventeen years ago I was an active addict and alcoholic who couldn't hold a pizza delivery job.

Courage Key #2. Belief

In order to dive beneath the surface and tap into your personal supply of courage, I think you have to believe in the cause or the event you're working toward. Yes, believing in yourself is important, but believing in what you're fighting for is equally essential. Martin Luther King, Jr., a shining example of courage, overcame great odds to fight for the civil rights cause in which he believed so fervently that he was willing to risk his life. When I look at my own life, I know that I so deeply believe in my sobriety that I would do anything I had to in order to protect it. And it is my experience with courage that keeps me strong. Even in those rare moments where I think a drink might be a good idea, I know with firm belief that a drink or a drug is never an option for me. My courage is one of the main tools that help keep me sober.

Courage Key #3. Faith

To become a successful leader you need faith. Faith in yourself, faith in the members of your team or committee, faith in your supervisors, and for some of you, faith in a Higher Being, whether you call that Higher Being God, Buddha, Jesus, Krishna, Allah, Karma, the Great Creator, the Great Spirit, or the Great Pumpkin. In my view, it doesn't matter what you call it as long as you recognize its existence and its ability to assist you. How many times have you been in just the right place at just the right time and something wonderful and magical happened?

As a leader, I know it is important for me to delegate some of the responsibilities of the group to other members. Sometimes this is very difficult and I need to muster all of my courage in order to let go. *Is that really a form of courage?* Yes. It takes courage to relinquish control. In reality, delegating authority strengthens the group and makes you a stronger leader. It requires courage not to take all of the responsibility on yourself. It takes courage to allow others to be a part of the process and to maintain your faith in the group and its members. For example, would Joe Montana, one of the greatest quarterbacks in football history, been as effective as a running back? Not a chance. A kicker or a linebacker? Of course not! The mere idea is absurd. Montana knew his position on the team and he had faith in the ability of his teammates to help him become a great leader, a winner of Super Bowls.

A number of years ago, I was working at a university in Northern California under a federal grant. When the grant ended, my position ended, leaving me unemployed. I looked all over California (which was my comfort zone) for a job, but couldn't find one. Looking beyond my comfort zone took courage and faith. I sent resumes to colleges in various parts of the country. Within a few weeks, I found an opening at a university in Virginia. I applied and was offered the position. Despite my initial fears I accepted the position and had faith that everything would work out. And indeed, my move to the East Coast was the start of many positive changes, including the one to become a full-time speaker. Faith will help you find courage.

Courage Key #4. Listen

Listen to your heart. Listen to that small voice inside that has been called your gut, your intuition or your inner-self. It doesn't matter what you call it as long as you recognize that it's there. Too often, we get caught up in thinking, spending so much time analyzing that we never move forward. We've all heard the stories of people who jump into action without thought, like the woman who lifts a car to free her trapped child. I talk to athletes about being in "the zone," and most of them say when they're in the zone, they play and react without thinking. It's about heart, it's about instinct and it's about courage.

Courage Key #5. Remain Teachable

M. Somerset Maugham said, "It wasn't until later in life I discovered how easy it is to say 'I don't know'." I believe three of the most courageous words known to man are "I don't know." It takes a courageous person to utter these words. It takes a great leader to stand in front of a group and admit he or she doesn't know. We all know that no one has all the answers. No one is perfect. And it is courage that allows us to say, "That's a good question. Let me get back to you on that." The wise leader knows his or her limitations and stays within them. A wise teacher is always a student first. It was a tough blow to my ego when I realized I couldn't save the world and I didn't have all the answers. But it was also such a relief! I let go of so much pressure when I accepted the fact that I needed other people to help me succeed. I know I am not the most organized person on the planet. My desk is a mess 90% of the time (OK, 95%). When I worked for the university I was able to hire an assistant, a highly organized and structured woman. I appreciated her and admired her for her ability to keep everything straight. And I made sure she knew how important she was to the success of the team.

Courage Builds Over Time

Tapping into your courage to make changes in the way you've always done things is not an easy task. And it's not something that happens overnight. A wise leader knows progress happens over time. An oak tree takes decades to reach its full height. A marathon runner trains for months or years before running the race. Although courage is something you already possess, it needs to be nurtured, explored and respected. Building courage takes practice. It won't happen on its own.

Remember that with practice comes progress. Be patient with yourself and with those around you. By trusting in the process, believing in yourself, having faith in a Being greater than yourself, listening to your instinct, and learning from the example of others, you will develop the courage necessary for successful leadership. I am a prime example of what can happen if you find your courage. I have gone from being a university dropout (actually a throw out) to a university administrator. Once fired from a job delivering pizza, today I am the president of my own company. I am living proof that anything is possible if you just get out of your own way. As you continue your journey, I wish you peace, happiness and, most of all, courage.

"A great deal of talent is lost to the world for want of a little courage. Every day sends to their graves obscure men whose timidity prevented them from making a first effort."

–Sydney Smith

CHAPTER SUMMARY

❑ Courage is found through action, not thought. You'll never know if you can accomplish a goal until you take the first steps toward achieving the goal.

❑ Be proactive rather than reactive. Courage is most effective as a proactive value. When you learn to harness its energy, so much more is open and available to you.

❑ To thine own self be true. Courage means being who you are rather than who you think other people want you to be. This is tough, but with time and practice, it is possible.

❑ Courage is about the process, not the result. Too often we get caught up judging our success by results. Many times the process is much more rewarding than the result.

❑ Get out of your own way! You'll be amazed at what you can do if you tap into your courage and not give in to your fears.

11

On Masterful Networking

The Voice of James Malinchak

"Why networking?" The answer is simple. It's not a coincidence that hundreds, even thousands, of people are hired for leadership positions over individuals more qualified and more experienced, merely because they have cultivated relationships with key centers of influence. It's not a coincidence that politicians are elected into office because they have cultivated relationships with more individual voters than their competitors. Through networking you will receive invitations that will expand your current knowledge base. Through networking you will be put in positions to expand your current skills and learn to communicate at many levels.

Networking is communicating with others to create quality, mutually beneficial relationships.

People often confuse networking with *quantity* of contacts. For the leader, this concept of networking defeats its very purpose—to enhance the *quality* of your contacts. The question is not how many people do you know, rather who do you know who can help you advance your cause or whose cause you can help to advance. Think of networking in terms of opening doors to the unknown. You might be tempted to believe the more doors that you have, the greater the odds you will make the right kinds of connections, right? Wrong. Networking is intentional by design. By placing yourself in situations that attract others with whom mutually beneficial relationships can be established, you increase the potential payoffs. Therefore, one of the greatest traits of the networking leader is their ability to actively identify what doors to open—not just how many doors.

Successful networking, however, also involves making something out of chance. Specifically, taking a coincidental encounter and fostering it into a mutually beneficial relationship is a networking characteristic that often gets over looked for a variety of reasons. Maybe the benefits aren't always obvious—or seem too far from your current scope of responsibility or reality. But, as I've learned from personal experience, you just never know. You need to overcome any fears or limiting beliefs that prevent you from taking advantage of chance encounters and have faith in the potential long term, as well as, short term benefits of your efforts. Consider the true story below.

Chances are you will run into someone of national celebrity once or twice in your lifetime. What you decide to do with that meeting is a reflection of the significance you put on networking. Do you ask for an autograph? Do you ask for a photo opportunity? Or do you remind yourself of the many values of networking? You will not always know how meeting someone of national exposure can possibly be an advantage to your role as leader. However, I learned how when I was presented with an opportunity to meet a famous author.

In the Company of Fame

Several years ago, when I was working as a full-time stockbroker, I received a call from a client named Cynthia. She and her husband, Michael, are movie writers and they had been in Cape Cod, Massachusetts for a few weeks working on a movie. They were turning a book written by Mary Higgins Clark in to a made for television movie. Cynthia invited my business partner Jase and I to visit with them for a few days on the Cape. She also said Mary had invited us to attend a private dinner party she was hosting at her house. I naturally accepted despite the fact that when I put down the phone I asked Jase, "Who is Mary Higgins Clark?"

To take advantage of opportunities that may or may not result from encounters with an author, for instance, you need to minimally know something about their work. You would ideally also like to know about their background, how they came to be a writer, and where they get their inspiration to write. Since we were scheduled to leave for the Cape only a few days later, I was forced, as you often will be, to do my homework quickly.

Networking Development Tips

Tip #1 – Do Your Homework

Because planning is a component of networking, you will need to make lists and seek out resources that can answer basic questions about the person or individuals you will be meeting. Some information will be more difficult to locate, but if you are willing to put in the time, you can learn what you need to about someone to make a good first impression. For instance, who knows the same person you are trying to meet? Who else works with this person? Where do they live? I'm not suggesting you stalk your potential pool of networking targets, rather you sit down and list what information might help increase the quality of your potential interactions.

Despite the many possible ways of learning more about my famous upcoming dinner host, time required that I select only a few methods of learning about Mary Higgins Clark. Step one was a trip to my local bookstore—a place of great networking resources. I asked the person working behind the counter if she had ever heard of an author named Mary Higgins Clark. She replied, "Oh yes," as she pointed to a display holding over ten of her books. Now I felt anxious. Despite my desire to read what appeared to be stacks upon stacks of her best-selling novels, I purchased only three to read on the plane. As I left the bookstore, I found myself less anxious and more excited about my upcoming encounter with such an established writer.

Tip #2 – Take the Initiative and Introduce Yourself

When meeting someone of notoriety, it is normal to act nervous or be concerned about making a bad first impression—despite your own level of success. However, even the most charismatic individuals say the wrong things out of nervousness or excitement. I think it's always wise to go for politeness. This seems like an obvious suggestion until you mistakenly call someone by their first name after a two-minute introduction. Whether the person you are approaching is famous or not, it's always acceptable to ask, "How would you like to be addressed?" after introducing yourself. I also like to have a few questions in mind that begin with the phrase, "Tell me about..." followed by a reference to something I know about the person. Because most people like to talk about themselves, the more the conversation places emphasis on who you are meeting—not why they should be thrilled to meet you—will most likely result in another encounter.

Fortunately, I didn't have to make any decisions about how to approach my dinner host, since Mary Higgins Clark greeted us as we approached her home. Still outside, Jase, Mary and I talked about a host of topics from our families and hobbies to the stock market. She was very interested in the market. She asked questions that, frankly, were rather complicated to answer. Instead of trying to impress her, a behavior mistakenly made by many trying to make a good impression, I employed a networking communication strategy of keeping it simple. So, we responded to her questions with simple, easy-to-understand answers.

Tip #3 – Make it About Them

As suggested above, you never want to try and make yourself sound better, smarter, more knowledgeable (even though you might be) than your partners in conversation. When you do this you come off as condescending, and despite your desire to build a foundation for additional interaction, you may have just closed the door. In fact, it is often your goal to ask more questions than you answer. Keep the other person engaged in the conversation by having them share information about themselves. Despite your position of leadership or status, find a common ground of interest. Lastly, do what is needed to make yourself appear approachable. Asking if it's alright to offer your business card is just one way to ensure this happens.

Much to my delight, my use of effective networking skills with Mary Higgins Clark was immediately rewarded. This does not always happen. In fact, some encounters represent the start and the end. For whatever reason, the attempt to follow-up and continue the relationship doesn't result in an on-going relationship. However, you'll never know unless you immediately begin making a more conscious effort to reach out. Because I have tried to make the skills and attitudes mentioned above part of my personality, I am particularly thrilled when there is an immediate result. For example, as Jase and I were leaving after a wonderful evening of conversation over a New England dinner, Mary asked if she could talk to us for a minute. We walked with her to the corner of the room where she said "I really like you guys and how easily you explained the answers to my questions. I'm looking to open another investment account with another company and I'd like to open the account with you."

Tip #4 – Stay in Frequent Contact

Mary, and her family, are still clients to this day and have become very good friends. Why? We took the initiative to stay in contact and follow-up with her. There are many ways you can do this as a leader. Writing thank you cards, sending holiday greetings, sending articles of interest with a note or remembering events of significance with flowers, are all examples of how to stay in frequent contact. Sending an e-mail message—although impersonal compared to a letter—also keeps your name and contact information out there. Call certain contacts periodically and if you happen to be in their area take them to lunch or at least give them a quick call to say hello. Effective leaders recognize the importance of staying in touch with those in their network.

Staying in Contact with a Childhood Friend

Let me give you another example of the payoffs of following up and staying in touch by telling you about a childhood friend. Michael and I played sports together in junior high school. After high school graduation our goals led us in separate directions. Mine led me to play college basketball in Ohio and Hawaii. Michael's goals led him to Detroit, where he began to train for a career as a professional boxer. We had not seen each for several years but I stayed in touch with him. After graduating from college, I began my career as a stockbroker in Los Angeles.

One day, I picked up a local newspaper and I read the following headline: "Evander Holyfield to Defend the World Heavyweight Boxing Title Against Michael Moorer." I couldn't believe it! This was my childhood friend. Immediately, I called a mutual friend of ours back in our small hometown of Monessen, Pennsylvania to ask if he knew how to get in touch with Michael because the fight was taking place the following week in Las Vegas. He did and gave me the telephone number to the room of one of Michael's bodyguards. I left a message and asked if he would have Michael return my call. Truthfully, I didn't think he would return my call because we hadn't seen each other for several years. Shortly thereafter, my telephone rang and it was Michael. He said he hadn't realized I was living in Los Angeles. More importantly, he said it was nice to hear from an old friend who stayed in touch all these years. He asked if I was planning on attending the fight. When I told him I would be there, he said to call him when I arrived so we could hopefully see each other.

To make a long story short, the night before the heavyweight title fight that would be broadcast to millions of viewers worldwide, I spent a few hours visiting with Michael in his hotel room. Since then, I have attended most of his fights and visited with him at the various training camps before each fight. Why? Simply because I took the initiative to stay in touch with someone I met in junior high school. If you are not making an effort to stay in touch with your contacts, then you could be missing many opportunities.

Tip #5 – Look for Ways to Offer Praise

Making others feel good is essential for walking through doors once they have been opened. Congratulating someone for their accomplishments or thanking them for taking the time to speak with you, are ways to praise. This does not mean you act like a crazed fan, rather you think about what you could say that would make the other person feel good about themselves. Praising your own accomplishments can lead to a competitive tone in your conversations. Having a calm sense of self while praising others makes you appear self-confident and much more worthy of additional contacts.

A Child Speaks Volumes

Recently, I was speaking in San Antonio, where my cousin, Davy Tyburski, lives. It had been several years since we had seen each other. Therefore, the invitation to stay at his house rather than in a hotel was warmly received. This would also give me a chance to visit with his wife and kids.

The night of my talk, Davy asked if he could bring his nine-year-old son, Kevin, because he wanted to begin exposing him to things that could be helpful to his future success. Naturally I agreed. However, I mentioned that Kevin probably wouldn't be able to relate to most of the information. Davy understood but wanted his son to attend nonetheless.

For about 90-minutes, I spoke about how to create a powerful network of contacts. One of the main points I emphasized was the importance of making others feel good about themselves. Among the variety of suggestions was to simply take the time to leave a note for someone praising them for something they did that day.

After the talk, Davy, Kevin and I stayed another hour-and-a-half so that I could answer questions and autograph books. Needless to say, it was now about 11:00 p.m. and past Kevin's bedtime. As a matter of fact, I noticed that Kevin was sleeping while I was answering questions and signing books. He continued to sleep on the ride home and as Davy and I helped him to his bedroom.

The next morning, I got out of bed and prepared to take a shower. As I opened the bedroom door, something caught my eye. A note with my name on it was taped to the door. It said, "Dear Cousin James, I just wanted to let you know that you did great last night. I can't wait to see you when I get home from school. Love, Kevin." Wow! I couldn't believe it! Kevin's simple gesture made me feel great and he motivated me to make an effort to leave more and more notes for others. If a nine-year-old can take such initiative to praise, grown leaders can certainly do the same.

Final Words

No successful leader has achieved their goals without the assistance of others. It doesn't matter how knowledgeable, qualified or experienced you are, without the assistance of others, you will most likely not excel. Networking can create a spider web effect by connecting you to opportunities. To lead effectively, you will need to stretch outside your immediate comfort zone to seek different ideas and discover a world of potential opportunities for yourself and your organization.

It doesn't matter how much leadership experience you have or what your leadership qualifications are, if you aren't focusing on creating quality, mutually beneficial relationships, others may not be receptive to your ideas.

Mastering the art of networking will enhance your leadership abilities and opportunities.

CHAPTER SUMMARY

❑ Being an effective leader requires expanding the quality of your contacts.

❑ You often never know the value of an initial interaction.

❑ It takes intentional thought to be an effective networker.

❑ Your first impression will determine how many additional interactions follow, but not always.

❑ There are five strategies that will enhance your abilities to become a master networker.

12

On Leaving a Legacy

The Voice of Charles Luke Latour, OP

A man found an eagle's egg and put it in the nest of a barnyard hen. The eaglet hatched with the brood of chicks and grew up with them—happy to be a chicken. All throughout his life the eagle did what the barnyard chickens did, thinking he was indeed a barnyard chicken. He scratched the earth for worms and insects. He clucked and cackled. And he would thrash his wings and fly a few feet into the air.

Years passed and the eagle grew very old. One day he saw a magnificent bird above him in the cloudless sky. It glided in graceful majesty among the powerful wind currents, with scarcely a beat of its strong golden wings.

The old eagle looked up in awe. "Who's that?" he asked.

"That's the eagle, the king of the birds," said his neighbor. "He belongs to the sky. We belong to the earth—we're chickens." So the eagle lived and died a chicken, for that's what he thought he was.

– Anthony S.J. DeMello in Awakening

The story is simple, yet its poignancy lies in how it parallels reality. Like the misguided eagle, far too many people fall short of their potential. Self-examination and introspection do not come easily.

It's hard work. We all need someone to help us discover our strengths, stretch us farther than we thought possible and challenge us to accomplish more. Leadership begins and ends with your commitment to this task.

The Importance of Leaving a Legacy

You and I know that visionary leaders, productive teams and vibrant organizations aren't born in and of themselves. On the contrary, they rely on the power of *legacy* to ensure the constant discovery and training of people and organizations. Legacies are created when leaders, like you, take the time and energy to help others develop their potential. Through encouragement, challenge and mentoring, you become the catalyst in their personal development. Your legacy will ensure the ongoing growth and success of your organization by creating future leaders through these challenges and developmental opportunities.

You have a responsibility to your organization and its members to assist in the development of their potential. Avoiding this responsibility has equally serious consequences. The key to accomplishing this depends on your interactions with your team members. You're called not just to lead, but to coach your organization's membership. The very essence of coaching is the one-to-one relationship between the coach and the coachee. Through this relationship the coach pushes, prods, challenges, teaches and encourages the individual in their discovery of hidden talent. The end-result not only affects the individual, but your entire team.

This chapter describes an exciting new paradigm for developing your organization and its membership—personal coaching. It focuses on how you assume this coaching role, and provides some outside resources for you to continue developing this new skill.

Coaching – It's Not Just for Jocks Anymore

Over the last few years, personal coaching has assumed a prominent and respected place within our culture. It provides a simple, yet highly effective process for facilitating individual growth and development. Mastering the required coaching skill-set not only benefits the individual being coached, but adds to your ability to effectively communicate. At its very heart, personal coaching focuses on the power and innate potential of the individual.

Coaching is designed to empower each individual to understand their potential and identify how they can maximize it. Through the development of a trust-based relationship with the coachee, the coach knows when to support and when to stretch, when to challenge and when to guide. The coach and coachee collaborate to set and achieve key development objectives, taking into account the needs of the organization as well as the skills and abilities of the individual. Through coaching, goals are developed and then broken down into manageable, measurable steps.

A coach is not a counselor, therapist,
consultant or personal guru.

The Philosophy of Coaching

Unlike other more conventional forms of counseling or advising, coaching avoids, at all costs, any scenario in which the coach assumes too prominent a role in the relationship. Your objective in the coaching process is to assist in the *transformation and evolution* of the individual. Your advice and wisdom play an important role, but always realizing that the focus remains on the coachee and his/her development.

What's in it for me? Integrating personal coaching into your leadership strategy will take more time and require more planning, more thought, and more dialogue on your part. There will be times, believe me, when you will question whether this is all worth the hassle. Then, why do it?

Ultimately, you do it because you care about the individual members of your organization *and* because you realize your organization is only as effective as its least effective member. Effective organizations are more productive and successful because:

- Goals are not only met, but surpassed.

- Team members want to stay on the team—less time recruiting and training new members.

- Your team constantly attracts individuals wanting to join— you get the best and the most talented.

- Your leadership abilities are recognized and rewarded.

Strong, empowered and motivated teams create an energy and enthusiasm that permeate the organization. They naturally produce new and innovative ideas. Your legacy of leadership consistently produces effective and satisfied members. All this just because you took a slightly different approach. Worth it? I think so.

Developing Your Coaching Skills

You have it in you to become a great personal coach. It's that simple. Don't get me wrong, to truly become an *exceptional* and *professional* coach you need proper training, experience and working with a coach of your own. But for you to begin coaching your team members, all you really need is the desire and the basic skill-set. An assortment of books and resources are available to help you continue developing your coaching skills.

Each coach is unique in their approach and style, but most strong coaches share some common traits:

- Enthusiasm

- Respect

- Caring

- Knowledge

These personal attributes create the foundation for a strong and successful coaching relationship. Let's take a moment and briefly examine specifically how these elements play such an important role in creating the coaching relationship.

Enthusiasm: Attitude, attitude, attitude! The outlook and attitude you convey about the coaching experience will directly impact the outcome. Whether you realize it or not, your team members often look to you to set the initial tone toward a project. So if you get excited, the individual being coached will catch the wave.

Respect: No one has completely reached their potential. Each of us is on a journey toward this goal; some more directly than others. As a coach, you are entering into a very vulnerable place with the coachee. Avoid using judgmental language. Don't allow your personal issues to cloud your responses.

Knowledge: Too much or too little of this will prove deadly. You're not a consultant. Your job is *not* to tell the coachee what to do. However, your wisdom and experience in a particular area is an important element in the relationship.

Care: Perhaps the most important, yet all too easily forgotten element. A genuine desire for the coachee's development and evolution should be the primary motivating factor in your desire to coach. You run into trouble when you begin to see each individual in a strictly clinical or utilitarian manner.

- Utilitarian centered: "I've got to get him more organized so he'll be able to meet the new team sales goals!" (*You* get what *you* need)

- Caring centered: "If we can figure out what motivates her, she'll be happier at work. If this fits into our team goals, she'll have greater motivation to meet the sales goals." (The process *begins and continues focusing on what's best for the individual.*)

As you can see, much of your coaching relationship relies upon these elements. Together they form the founding principles underlying a strong coaching relationship:

1. Trust between the coach and the coachee.
2. Mutual respect based on trust and built by a genuine sense of commitment to the process.

3. A desire to maximize potential.

4. Commitment (time and energy).

First and foremost of these principles is trust—a trait of leadership mentioned throughout this book. *Trust is the heart of the coaching relationship.* The earlier you understand the primacy of trust in the coaching relationship, the sooner you will begin to see tangible results from the coaching experience. Without trust he/she will constantly filter or hedge his/her responses. This veiled honesty ultimately affects your ability to question, challenge and move the individual forward.

Trust cannot be forced. It needs to spring naturally from the relationship. The coachee will look to your past and present attitude, outlook, and actions in determining their level of trust. They must find in you a real desire for their general and professional fulfillment.

Try some of these suggestions to help the trust process get off to a good start:

- Set the ground rules in the first few meetings. How often will you meet? How long? What, if any, are the parameters regarding topics?

- Let the coachee know you value their privacy and that anything discussed during your coaching session will remain confidential.

- Let the coachee know you are there to help them discover greater satisfaction from the team.

THE COACHING SKILL-SET

Getting Down to Business

Evolving as an effective leader requires you to develop a toolbox of skills. Like many tools, these skills serve many purposes and can be used in a variety circumstances. The five basic skills you need to master in order to develop as a truly effective coach are:

- Listening
- Discovery
- Challenging
- Visioning
- Assigning

Most of these skills are foundational for any leader. The fact that you are reading this book indicates you probably are well beyond an introductory stage of leadership and thus understand the basic concepts underlying each of these skills. In the discussion that follows I will explain the use of each skill without repeating much of the information you already know—or that has already been discussed in previous chapters. Although you may have some understanding of these skills, their uses in coaching require a much greater proficiency. I cannot encourage you strongly enough to continue training in the use of these skills.

Listening:

Some people believe the art of *listening* has gone the way of acid washed jeans and Farrah Fawcett hairstyles. Your coaching relationship begins with your ability to listen attentively and actively to what the coachee is *really* saying. This requires practice and *intentionality* on your part. There are five key elements to effective listening. Use these to help you develop this skill:

1. *Stay in the present*: Focus on what the coachee is saying here and now. Avoid letting your mind wander to other things. This requires you to listen actively and follow-up with appropriate questions.

2. *Clarify when you don't understand*: Don't be afraid to request clarification when you don't fully understand what the coachee is attempting to convey. Ask for clarification.

3. *Trust your gut*: Active listening requires you to trust your inner intuition. Listen to what it's telling you. Often we

don't consciously catch the body language and subtle messages people send. Our intuition is often the response to those subtle messages.

4. *Utilize quiet moments sparingly:* Quiet moments are often good times for the coachee and the coach to digest portions of a challenging conversation. However, feel free to encourage the coachee to talk when you feel the silence is disruptive or an escape.

5. *Keep eye contact:* One of the most important ways to let someone know you're listening is to keep eye contact with them. This does not mean staring intently into their eyes. Rather, keep your eyes casually focused on the bridge above their eyes.

Discovery:

Discovery provides context to what you hear. Learning to develop questions that require the coachee to reflect and examine is one of the most important coaching skills. The questions are like a mirror, constantly forcing the coachee to examine their perspectives and outlooks. They are pivotal to the self-examination process.

Formulating intuitive questions takes time, training and practice. Remember, the goal of discovery is to get the coachee to open up about themselves. Listed below are some tips to help you begin mastering this skill:

1. *Use open-ended questions:* Open-ended questions allow for discussion. They cannot be answered in a one word response. Their purpose is to elicit deeper discussion and clarity to a situation/discussion. E.g., "What are some specific examples of how Bob has dropped the ball on this project?"

2. *Know when to use "how" and "why" questions:* "How" questions usually involve seeking information about doing something. "Why" questions usually involve seeking

information about something that was already done. E.g., "How could you have handled the situation so your team could have accomplished their goals?"

3. *Have the coachee begin by describing specific moments*: One great way to get conversation moving and the coachee relaxed is to ask them to describe a time in their life when they succeeded at something. Have them describe the moment and the feeling. See if they can translate the event to the current situation.

Challenging:

There will be times when you'll want to *challenge* the coachee. Challenging takes many forms, each with a specific end in mind. Basically, challenging is a request or question you ask the coachee that requires them to push themselves farther and deeper than ever before. As a coach, you should be constantly looking for ways in which you can "raise the bar" of expectations. You do this so the coachee needs to dig deep to find those hidden abilities otherwise left undiscovered and unused.

It should be noted, however, that the purpose and use of the challenging process must always focus on building the coachee's confidence and self-awareness. Never set the coachee up for failure through the use of a challenge.

Challenges can take any number of forms. Some examples of challenges include:

- Assign the coachee some form of "fieldwork" to be completed before the next coaching session to help reinforce or develop a needed skill.

- Ask a question that cuts to the heart of the matter.

- Constantly "raise the bar" of expectations—realize that many of us don't push ourselves hard enough. As a result, we never know how truly great we can be.

- Keep your coachee accountable to what they say and do. Keep demanding a high level of integrity and commitment.

- Require that the coachee verbalize their accomplishments with you. Make sure they celebrate as much as they complain when they don't meet their expectations.

- Don't just moan failure. Dig into the reasons why with the coachee. Then have them list five things they learned from the situation.

Visioning:

There are times in our lives when we all lose perspective. We get so caught up in the moment that we lose sight of the bigger picture and our place in it. Some of what the coach does with the coachee revolves around helping him/her see the forest in spite of the trees. This requires the coach to keep his or her own perspective and not get caught up in the coachee's issues. Some level of detachment is both healthy and necessary if you are to really assist the coachee in discovering their distinct skills and abilities.

Ways to help the coachee in the vision development process:

- Ask them to list their strengths (personal, professional and academic).

- Take on the role of being their fan when they need assistance with appreciating what they do well.

- Help them set goals. Stack them at three levels—(1) Attainable, (2) Needs some work, but can be done, (3) A stretch, but with some major work coachee can reach it.

- Have them assess their current life from all angles—personal, professional, social, religious/spiritual, educational, family, goals. Rank each from one to ten. Have them choose one area and list the specific steps needed to improve that area by two points. Chart their efforts so they can see their progress.

Assigning:

"Fieldwork" is usually the first and the final topic you and the coachee discuss each coaching session. Think of fieldwork as a homework *assignment* you give the coachee to help them strengthen a particular area, develop a particular skill or put into action something you had discussed earlier. Fieldwork should be challenging and ample enough to keep the coachee focused on a particular area. Caution should be taken so you don't over assign fieldwork. This only leads to the coachee spending an inadequate amount of time on the fieldwork or not doing it at all.

Creating fieldwork that both challenges the coachee and incorporates the issues discussed during the coaching session requires quite a bit of practice and finesse. Some examples of fieldwork are listed below. Feel free to use them as a template for your own coaching fieldwork.

- Find at least ten separate situations over the next few weeks where you are asked to do something. Say "No!" Record how it feels? Does it get any easier?

- Practice a mock office conflict situation with someone you know well. Use a situation that actually happened. Try out three different approaches based on the conflict resolution models we discussed.

- List the ten things you would continue doing even if you had won the lottery and working was no longer necessary. Next to the jobs you listed—write "yes" if pursuing it would be feasible at this time. Consider income and education. Choose the top five. Then, the top three. What obstacles keep you from pursuing these jobs? Create a long-range plan for securing one of these jobs.

There you have them; the five basic coaching skills. A professional coach has a toolbox loaded with other more precise skills-sets. These come with training and practice. However, with these basic five under your belt, you can immediately begin utilizing coaching as a part of your leadership strategy.

"There is something that is much more scarce,
something rarer than ability.
It is the ability to recognize ability."

— Robert Half

The Coaching Session

Creating the environment for a good coaching session requires some mental pre-planning, but the difference it makes cannot be underscored. The coaching session requires five basic keys:

- Decide on a purpose for the coaching.
- Speak plainly and clearly.
- Stay on task and avoid discussions that lead to nowhere.
- Realize the discussion may take turns you had not planned.
- Avoid making assumptions.

These keys should provide you with a context from which you can plan your coaching sessions. However, it's been my experience that some of those new to coaching need some help in organizing the basic structure of the coaching session. So, very briefly the structural framework for a one-hour coaching session is as follows:

1. Welcome and pleasantries.
2. Review what was discussed last time you met.
3. Discuss any fieldwork assigned.
4. Review areas of accomplishment and failure since the last session.
5. Discuss the pre-determined issue(s) for this particular session.
6. Assign fieldwork.
7. Closing.

Each session will be different, based on the coachee's individual needs. In general, your duties as a coach include, listening to where the coachee is at, asking questions to clarify or evoke further information, give feedback, brainstorm ideas and challenge the coachee, offering encouragement, helping them in finding the lesson in failures and mistakes, and helping the coachee see the big picture.

This probably looks pretty daunting, but it actually comes quite naturally once you get used to it. The key is to go over the session a few times in your mind before your first few meetings. Make sure you've reviewed their coaching preparation form and relax. You have gotten this far by luck. Trust yourself.

The Opportunity Before You

Let's take a moment and revisit the story at the beginning of this chapter. By just adding these lines in the middle of the story, the eagle's life changes fundamentally.

> *One day, after his first year, the leader of the chicken community approached the eagle and said, "You seem to be having some trouble flapping your wings and laying the eggs. Yet, I see so much more potential in you. You have a lot to give this community. Why don't we meet and talk about it tomorrow."*

The eagle's life would never have been the same again. Rather than living his life never realizing his true potential, the eagle would have known the freedom of flight and power he possessed by right of his birth.

The power of legacy relies on the commitment of individual leaders like you to make a difference. Successful leaders have always focused on more than the finish line. They instinctively knew the source of an organization's success lies in the continuity and quality of its leadership. Coaching provides you with the means to achieve both.

*"The achievements of an organization are the results
of the combined effort of each individual."*

— Vince Lombardi

CHAPTER SUMMARY

❑ Legacies are created when leaders take the time and energy to help others develop their potential.

❑ Coaching involves a one-to-one relationship between the coach and the "coachee."

❑ There are fundamental principles of coaching.

❑ The coaching skill-set includes listening, discovery, challenging, visioning and assigning.

❑ The power of a legacy depends upon the individual leader's commitment to make a difference and take those around them to higher places of development.

The Voices

• •

Authors Biographies and Contact Information

Leaders from all corners of the country have called upon **Rick Barnes** to deliver powerful messages in a practical, approachable style. Rick has served numerous leadership roles through international associations and has over 18 years experience in higher education. Rick has been a member of the faculty for leadership conferences across the country and has been a featured speaker on more than 150 college campuses. Leadership training, retreats, challenge course facilitation, workshops, seminars, and keynotes. Rick has done them all! An established speaker, author and educator, Rick can be contacted at www.campuspeak.com/barnes/htm or call 817-788-5019.

David Coleman is best known nationwide as The Dating Doctor. He is a sought after speaker, trainer and retreat facilitator at corporations, colleges, churches and civic organizations. David is an established author, newspaper columnist, talk radio show host, and has been a featured guest on radio and television stations coast to coast. Over 1,000,000 people in all 50 states (and Canada) have experienced his energetic and entertaining programs. He has been named National Speaker of the Year on six occasions. David can be contacted at or at www.datingdoctor.com or call 513-583-8000.

For over 20 years, **Doug Cureton** has been engaged in the education, training, and development of organizations ranging from college and universities to corporations and federal government agencies including the FBI and the CIA. Doug is the founder and senior consultant for CreativiTEAM, Inc. He is a sought after speaker, trainer and facilitator at many national and international conferences presenting keynote addresses, workshops, retreats and training seminars. Doug can be contacted via e-mail at kre8ive@aol.com or at his website at www.CreativiTEAM.com or call 954-522-5883.

Lenny Dave energizes, informs and entertains corporate and college audiences with his fun, motivational keynotes and workshops. In an active learning environment, he emphasizes the fundamental concepts of creativity, leadership, success and wellness—all with the goal of helping to move individuals and organizations forward. Lenny's background in the field of creative communications, combined with his talent as a humorist and motivational public speaker, have enabled him to serve a diverse client base. He believes that learning can and should be fun! President and founder of Lenmar Communications in Cincinnati, Lenny can be contacted at www.creativity123.com or call 513-791-4149.

His dynamic and inspirational presentations have touched the lives of thousands of people from around North America since 1986. **Randy Haveson** is experienced as a counselor, a university administrator, and a successful speaker. His addictions to cocaine and alcohol led him to a heart attack at 21, expulsion from college, and a serious suicide contemplation in 1984. Today Randy has a Master's degree in counseling and has received national recognition for the work he has done on college campuses. Randy works with university and high school students, but also with business and corporate professionals on the topics of team building, self-esteem, and substance abuse in the workplace. Randy can be reached through his website at www.randyspeaks.com or call 404-252-7360.

Delivering a motivating message is **Kathy Humphrey's** aim every time she graces the platform as a speaker. She is also very skilled at leading sessions with administrators, managers, faculty and today's college students. Kathy has worked in higher education for nearly two decades. She currently serves as the Vice President for Student Development at Saint Louis University. She has served as a keynote speaker and consultant for colleges, universities, churches, national and regional associations, and government agencies throughout North America. To contact Kathy call 314-977-2226 or SunshineKathyH@aol.com.

Nancy Hunter Denney is a nationally recognized motivational speaker, educator and author specializing in higher education, non-profit helping organizations and motivational keynotes for corporations. She has touched the lives of hundreds of thousands of individuals with her high energy, insightful and inspiring original thoughts on life and leadership. Her philosophy on life is summed up in her own words, *"How you spend your time is the only true measurement of your priorities in life."* Nancy has appeared on numerous national, regional and local radio and TV shows discussing her first motivational book, *Life by Design.* She has also created numerous inspirational posters and products including *The Future is Yours to Create!* video—all of which are available on her on-line store. For more information about Nancy Hunter Denney contact www.nancyhunterdenney.com or call 888-566-7536.

Will Keim has lectured to 2 million students from 1000 college campuses. His corporate clients include AT&T, IBM, Delta Air Lines, State Farm Insurance, and Kinko's. He has been awarded the prestigious Paul Harris Fellow from Rotary International for "efforts to create understanding and cooperation among the world's peoples." He holds two national awards for interfraternalism. Dr. Keim is the author of six books, travels extensively to "listen and lecture," and lives in Corvallis, Oregon with his wife and four children. Will can be contacted at www.willkeim.com or call 800-848-3897.

Charles Luke Latour, OP has been active in the area of leadership development for over 10 years. Both as speaker and consultant, he has impacted the lives of educators and students in schools across America, Canada and England. Charles has presented keynote speeches at a host of professional development conferences within higher education. Recently, Charles has focused on integrating personal coaching and leadership development strategies. With degrees in law and theology, he brings an innovative approach to leadership development. A member of the Dominican Southern Province, Charles is currently the Associate Dean of Students for the University of Dallas in Irving, Texas. He can be reached at www.charleslatour.com and www.leaderville.net or call 972-721-5113.

James Malinchak has delivered over 1,100 motivational presentations at corporate meetings, association conferences, youth conferences and colleges worldwide. He has appeared in *USA Today*, *The Wall Street Journal* and several hundred other publications. Currently James owns three businesses, has authored eight books and has read and researched over 1,500 books on personal and professional development. A Contributing Author to the #1 Best-selling book series *Chicken Soup for the Soul®*, James delivers high content messages that "Empower Audiences to Achieve Extraordinary Results!" James can be contacted at www.Malinchak.com or call 888-793-1196, or e-mail JamesMal@aol.com.

Joe Martin is a nationally known speaker, respected university professor, author, and educational consultant. Specializing in service and retention, Joe has presented for more than 500 different associations, corporations, colleges and universities, helping hundreds of thousands of staff members, educators, and students maximize their leadership potential. As the host of his own television talk show and the founder and president of RealWorld University, Joe has been regarded as one of "America's Top Motivational Professors." He currently teaches public relations and business communication at the University of West Florida in Pensacola. You can contact Joe at www.RWuniversity.com or call 850-212-0227, or by e-mail at NoExqse@aol.com.

Known as the "High Tech" motivator, **Marlon Smith** received his B.S. in Electrical Engineering from the University of Virginia. He has worked for two Fortune-500 corporations, IBM and Hewlett-Packard. Through high-energy multimedia presentations, Marlon has spoken in 43 of the United States, six other countries, and has been featured on television. He is also an accomplished author, contributing to the *Chicken Soup* series and writing his own book, *"What's Up?—Solution Guide for Today's Young People."* Marlon may be contacted at www.successbychoice.com or 800-321-2464.

Author Resources

By David Coleman

The following resources are available for viewing and ordering through The Dating Doctor's on line store at www.datingdoctor.com or by calling 513-583-8000. All forms of payment are accepted.

- ❑ **Date Smart! How to Stop Revolving and Start Evolving in Your Relationships.** Prima Publishing Simon and Schuster
- ❑ *Prescriptions from The Dating Doctor Booklet.* Coleman Productions Publisher
- ❑ *Pick-Up Line* T-shirts

By Lenny Dave

The following products are available as conversation starters and can be ordered on www.creativity123.com or by calling 513-791-4149:

- ❑ "But We've Always Done It This Way" (with red slash mark) on 3" round buttons
- ❑ "But We've Always Done It This Way" 16oz. white acrylic hot/cold mugs

By Nancy Hunter Denney

The following resources and products are available for viewing and ordering through Nancy's on-line store at www.nancyhunterdenney.com or by calling 888-565-7536. All forms of payment are accepted.

- ❑ **Life by Design: A Do-It-Yourself Approach for Achieving Happiness.** Victory, Inc. Publishers (see www.lifebydesignbook.com or Amazon.com)
- ❑ *The Future is Yours to Create!* six minute inspirational video
- ❑ *The Future is Yours to Create!* staff T-shirts
- ❑ *The Future is Yours to Create!* 11"x17" full color poster
- ❑ *One on One* 8"x11" full color poster
- ❑ *Life by Design* 11"x17" full color poster
- ❑ *You Make a Difference* 11"x17" poster
- ❑ *You Make a Difference* 16oz coffee mug with inspirational saying
- ❑ *You Make a Difference* professional pens

By Will Keim, Ph.D.

The following books are available for ordering on www.willkeim.com or directly from the publishers or by calling 800-848-3897:

- ❑ **The Education of Character: Lessons for Beginners.** Harcourt Brace Publishers
- ❑ **Spirit Journey.** Chalice Press Publisher

- ❏ **Life After College: Lessons for Students in Transition.** Chalice Press Publisher
- ❏ **The Truth About College: 50 Lessons for Parents Before They Start Writing Checks.** Chalice Press Publisher
- ❏ **The Tao of Christ: The Way of Love for a World of Hurt.** Viaticum Press Publisher
- ❏ **The Sayings of W.S. Keim.** Viaticum Press Publisher

By Charles Luke Latour, OP

The following on-line e-zine contains updated information, resources and articles on personal and professional development opportunities and leadership. (Co-hosted by Will Keim, Ph.D. and Charles Luke Latour)

- ❏ *www.leaderville.net*
- ❏ *The Leading Buzz – to subscribe go to www.leaderville.net*
- ❏ *The Naked Leader – to subscribe go to www.leaderville.net*

By James Malinchak

The following resources were produced by James Malinchak International and are available on www.malinchak.com or by calling 888-793-1196.

- ❏ **Success Starts With Attitude: 50 Ways to Refuel, Recharge and Reenergize Yourself in Business and Life.**
- ❏ **How to Be a Master Networker: 7 Secrets for Getting What You Want Through Who You Know** (Co-Author Joe Martin).
- ❏ **Live With Purpose, Passion and Power: 9 Action Steps for Creating Extraordinary Business and Personal Results** (Co-Author Joe Martin).
- ❏ **Teenagers Tips for Success: Create a Future, Achieve Your Dreams and Become Very Successful**
- ❏ **From College to the Real World: Street-Smart Strategies for Landing Your Dream Job and Creating a Successful Future**
- ❏ *Network Your Way to Success – 7 Secrets for Building Powerful and Profitable Contacts* (6 cassettes)
- ❏ *James Malinchak Live!* (Volume 1: Motivation)
- ❏ *James Malinchak Live!* (Volume 2: Inspiration)
- ❏ *Jump Start Your Speaking Career* (2 cassettes)
- ❏ *How to Ace College and Land a Great Career* (Co-recorded with Joe Martin) (6 cassettes)

By Joe Martin

The following audiotapes are available for ordering by calling 850-212-0227. In addition, books and audiotapes co-authored with James Malinchak are listed above.

- ❏ *Give and Grow Rich: Success Strategies for Servant Leaders*
- ❏ *Get a Grip: Taking Control of Your Mental and Emotional Attitude*

TO ORDER DISCOUNTED BULK QUANTITIES OF

Let Your Leadership Speak: How to Lead and Be Heard

CONTACT THE PROJECT COORDINATOR AT:

The Future is Yours to Create! Company
50 Richards Avenue
Paxton, MA 01612
888-566-7536